Bob Mc Geady has been involved in the Planning and Local Government field for over 40 years. He initially spent 17 years working for various local authorities. In that time he has dealt with a multitude of planning matters ranging from large-scale retail and housing developments to discrete one off proposals. He moved to Private Practice in 2000 and was a partner and Head of Planning and Commercial Property at Kester Cunningham John, leading a team that dealt with all aspects of commercial development.

He is now a consultant at Ashtonslegal and continues to act for local authorities as well as private clients and objectors. He regularly provides training sessions for officers and members of various local authorities as well as speaking at events organised by such bodies as the Local Government Group and the Royal Town Planning Institute and MBL Seminars.

Bob was an Independent Board Member of a large regional housing association and chaired a regional homelessness charity. He is currently a member of a local housing association. In the Legal 500 and Chambers Directory he is rated as a leading individual for planning in East Anglia. Clients also say that he 'has a valuable insight into the attitudes and even the politics of planners' with another describing him as "a star in the firmament of planning lawyers."

Chambers and Partners Directory said of Meyric Lewis KC that "*what Meyric doesn't know about planning law isn't worth knowing*". He is listed by the Legal 500 in the first rank of KCs in the categories of Planning and Local Government Law. He specialises in all aspects of planning, compulsory purchase and environmental law both at inquiries and in the courts at all appellate levels. His clients range from substantial developers to public authorities and individual developers and objectors.

Certificates of Lawful Use and Development: A Guide to Making and Determining Applications

Second Edition

Certificates of Lawful Use and Development: A Guide to Making and Determining Applications

Second Edition

Bob Mc Geady B.A. (Hons) Dip. L.G.
Solicitor (Retired)
Consultant Planning and local government related matters

Meyric Lewis KC, B.A. (Hons)
Diploma in Law
Barrister

Law Brief Publishing

Published 2024 by Law Brief Publishing, an imprint of Law Brief Publishing Ltd
30 The Parks
Minehead
Somerset
TA24 8BT

www.lawbriefpublishing.com

Paperback: 978-1-916698-51-2

PREFACE

The first edition of this book had been milling around in Bob Mc Geady's head for quite some time. It is based on the successful courses he led for more than 10 years on the subject which have been widely praised for their clear and practical approach. This book develops this in more detail and is intended to provide a template for everyone faced with either making or having to decide an application.

Bob and Meyric have worked together for over 30 years on many major projects and have spoken together on various planning related topics. Meyric's work on enforcement with the Association of Enforcement Officers made him a natural writing partner for what had become of those tasks that seemed straightforward but needed some impetus to get going.

Both Bob and Meyric hope that this book – now in its second edition – will be of practical benefit to those who use it and that the checklists at the end of each chapter will stimulate the thought processes of those involved at different stages of the application.

Since the first edition, we have included a new chapter on Caravans and Mobile Homes which give rise to their own specific issues.

The law stated is based on information available to us on 30 September 2024.

Bob McGeady
Meyric Lewis KC
October 2024

PREFACE

CONTENTS

INTRODUCTION

At its simplest this book concerns two sections of the Town and Country Planning Act 1990. That would, however, do the topic a disservice as there are a number of other sections that are engaged including the definition of development as well as the obvious link with the sections concerning enforcement notices and breach of condition notices. We will explore these links where appropriate.

One might be prompted to ask why these provisions are important at all given their apparent lack of influence other than in limited circumstances. Such an approach underestimates the importance of the provisions especially when considered in the light of the developing case law concerning the lawful commencement of development where certain conditions have not been discharged in advance. Following the financial crash lenders have placed more pressure on those who advise them as to valuation and title issues and are seeking active warranties from surveyors, planning consultants and lawyers that the use to which property is to be put, and upon which valuation assumptions have been made, is lawful so that the security over the property is not illusory. Certificates of Lawfulness both as to existing and proposed use have a very important part to play in this process where there are any doubts as to the planning status of the land. It is likely that more applications will at least be considered if not submitted given this approach.

As the legislation and guidance makes clear there is no need to make a formal application for a certificate once the relevant period for acquiring immunity has expired and it may be that applying the practical steps advocated in the book lead to a conclusion that an application is unnecessary but nevertheless the process and questioning approach should, at the very least be engaged so that those tasked with advising can advise with confidence.

Where an enforcement notice has been issued it is possible to appeal on the basis that the time period for taking enforcement action has expired and an Inspector considering such an appeal can issue a certificate if satisfied that at the date that the appeal is lodged the relevant time period has expired and the development has thus become immune from enforcement action. An Inspector cannot, if only dealing with an appeal against an enforcement notice, issue a Certificate unless there is a conjoined appeal where an application for a certificate was made and refused and an appeal is then lodged at the same time as the enforcement appeal. The evidence required and the questions to be asked when dealing with the enforcement appeal are the same as those engaged in the process of seeking a certificate.

This book takes the subjects in a logical sequence and builds from the basic definition of development through to determining applications and dealing with appeals. At the end of each topic is a checklist for matters that should be considered and to act as an aide memoire for those to engaged at the appropriate part of the process. The authors hope that by using these guides those who do not deal with the subject regularly, and those who do, will be able approach the task with confidence and thus be able to advise on the issues armed with a more measured approach to evidence and procedure.

CHAPTER ONE

THE BASICS OF A CERTIFICATE OF LAWFULNESS OF EXISTING USE AND DEVELOPMENT

Section 191 of the Town and Country Planning Act 1990 envisages 3 circumstances where a certificate may be issued. Two relate to unauthorized development and the third relates to development in breach of a condition. Subsection (1) of Section 191 provides as follows;

> *"If any person wishes to ascertain whether-*
>
> *(a) any existing use of buildings or other land is lawful;*
>
> *(b) any operations which have been carried out in, on, over or under land are lawful; or*
>
> *(c) any other matter constituting a failure to comply with any condition or limitation subject to which planning permission has been granted is lawful,*
>
> *he may make an application for the purpose to the local planning authority specifying the land and describing the use, operations or other matter."*

The first question that therefore needs to be asked is "What type of development are we concerned with?" This question is more than academic as we shall see, as there are different time limits that apply depending upon the form of development involved. Just to complicate matters it may be necessary to engage both forms when seeking a certificate.

So what does development entail? The answer is provided by section 55(1) of the Town and Country Planning Act 1990. This provides as follows;

> *"Subject to the following provisions of this section, in this Act, except where the context otherwise requires, "development" means the carrying out of building, engineering, mining or other operations in, on, over or under land, or the making of any material change in the use of buildings or other land"*

Before we explore the issues associated with the different forms of development it is necessary to remind ourselves that there are various matters that do not constitute development. These are contained in subsection 2. This includes such things as development undertaken in reliance on permitted development rights. There was an indication in Annex 8 of Circular 10/97 that a certificate could be granted in respect of such development. This is continued in paragraph 011 of the NPPG which states that "*a lawful development certificate can be granted on the basis that there is an extant planning permission….*" However, the question has to be asked how development can become lawful on the expiry of the relevant time limit for taking enforcement action when to undertake the development in the first place did not require planning permission. If there is any doubt as to whether or not such development is lawful then an appropriate application would be for a Certificate of Lawfulness of Proposed Use or Development (CLOPUD) where a certificate can establish that it would be lawful to retain the development or to continue to use it on the basis that permission was deemed to have been granted for the development to have been constructed or used in the first place.

An example of this is *Eatherley*, "the basement case" ie *Eatherley v. London Borough of Camden* [2016] EWHC 3108 (Admin) in which the requirement for planning permission in relation to the creation of a basement beneath a residential dwellinghouse was tested in the courts. In *Eatherley*, the householder wished to establish that excavation of a basement beneath his home was covered by the general permission granted by article 3(1) and Class A in Part 1 of Schedule 2 to the GPDO 2015 for development involving "the enlargement, improvement or other alteration of a dwellinghouse". This was against the background of the controversy caused in London in particular by the disruption caused by people enlarging their houses by digging out extra living space at basement level. The Council duly granted the householder a CLOPUD under section 192 but this was challenged by a neighbour, Mr Eatherley. The main argument on the construction of the GPDO succeeded but the certificate was quashed on a detailed point on the facts.

The most recent guidance as contained in the National Planning Policy Guidance is unclear. Paragraph 003 of the relevant part of the Guidance provides the current guidance. It says;

> *"In summary, lawful development is development against which no enforcement may be taken and where no enforcement notice is in force, or for which planning permission is not required."*

Paragraph 003 is non-specific as to whether it is only referring to CLEUDS or whether it includes or is limited to CLOPUDS. The situation seems to the writers to remain the same in that if permission was not required in the first place then the appropriate means for establishing lawfulness is via a CLOPUD rather than a CLEUD.

The simple question therefore seems to be to establish what development is involved and whether or not an enforcement notice is in force. In this respect it is important to remember that for the purposes of section 191 an enforcement notice also includes a Breach of Condition Notice, see section 191(3)(b) However, just because there is an enforcement notice does not automatically mean that a claim for immunity will fail as the actual breach for which a certificate is sought may not be a breach of the enforcement at all. This is why it is so important to look at the precise contents of enforcement notices and see how it relates to the use or development that is now alleged to be immune. The two may not exactly correlate and there could be a situation where a further breach has occurred that the council thought was covered by the enforcement notice but in reality it hadn't been. For example, if an enforcement notice prohibited the sale and display of cars but the use then changed to the storage of cars for sale elsewhere and the council did not get around to taking action or were unsuccessful in a prosecution the claim for immunity could be made out if a further enforcement notice has not been served.

The second element here is the requirement for the enforcement notice to be "in force". It is necessary to consider situations where a notice had been complied with or has even been withdrawn. Whilst compliance with a notice will ensure that subsequent development of the same kind will be prevented by the issued enforcement notice it is not unknown for LPAs to withdraw notices when they perceive there has been compliance without thinking about the long term consequences. When undertaking due diligence on a site solicitors will often ask for historic enforcement notices to be removed. Provided a risk-based approach is taken by local authorities this should not cause undue difficulty. For example, if the land subject to the enforcement notice has been subsumed into a much larger site which has then been re-developed then the removal of the enforcement notice will not cause any difficulties. However, if the site remains as when the notice was issued then removal will have more implications for the future.

In relation to whether an enforcement notice is "in force" paragraph 003 further states;

> *"An enforcement notice is not in force where an enforcement appeal is outstanding or an appeal has been upheld and the decision has been remitted to the Secretary of State for redetermination, but that redetermination is still outstanding".*

Looking at the interaction of enforcement notices and CLEUDS the case of *R v Challinor [2007] EWCA Crim 2102* deals with the situation. In the Challinor case the landowner was prosecuted for breaching an enforcement notice. He tried to rely on the fact that a certificate had been granted for part of the site affected by the Enforcement notice. The Court of Appeal held he could not challenge validity of notice other than by appeal in normal way under section 174 of the Planning Act 1990. Therefore, if you are confronted by such a situation you will need to ensure that you check the position as regards the notice and the certificate.

Section 191 is also concerned with breaches of condition. Whilst it will be fairly clear as to whether or not there is a breach of condition one issue that might arise is whether or not the condition itself is valid. The case of *Basingstoke and Deane v Secretary of State [2009] EWHC 1012 (Admin)* dealt with the question as to whether or not the imposition of a condition could be revisited. In that case an application was made for two agricultural workers cottages. The condition restricting the use of the cottages to agricultural workers was imposed at the request of the applicant in order to avoid paying a development charge. The properties had a chequered use with breaches of the condition from time to time. A certificate was applied for and granted on appeal by an Inspector on the basis that there could not have been a breach of the condition as it had been invalid from the outset.

The council challenged the decision on the basis that the condition was one that could have been properly imposed and could thus attract enforcement action. The court held that the condition was capable of being a proper condition. However, the reasons why a condition were imposed were of considerable importance[1] and in this case as the condition was not imposed for proper planning purpose it was invalid.

In such circumstances, an applicant may be able to succeed in an application for a CLEUD on the basis that the development was carried out unlawfully having been implemented in breach of a condition precedent and so the development carried out is not subject to the conditions originally imposed on the planning permission for it (which was not complied with). This may be significant in particular where planning permission is granted for a dwelling subject to a restriction on occupancy. If the development was not lawfully implemented, then the occupancy restriction will not "bite". It needs to be borne in mind, however, that the use of such a dwelling will not automatically be lawful. We discuss this aspect further with reference to the Welwyn Hatfield case below.

This case is likely to lead to more scrutiny of conditions when either enforcement action is contemplated or a landowner is considering an application where there may or may not have been a breach of condition. The fact that planning permissions in the modern era have to specify reasons for the imposition of conditions will make life a bit easier but there may still be a need to go through the planning file and even seek information from previous landowners and applicants.

Pre-Commencement Conditions and Commencement

A major area for debate where conditions are concerned is the situation where planning permission was granted subject to conditions to the effect the "no development shall commence" unless and until certain pre-conditions have been satisfied, requiring prior approval of

1 See *Crisp from The Fens v Rutland CC (1950) 114 J.P. 105*

some aspect of the development before it can start. It often happens that development is commenced before a particular condition in that (or similar) form has been discharged and so the question arises whether the commencement of development was unlawful as being carried out in breach of condition so that the development itself does not benefit from planning permission.

The courts have long taken the view that works carried out in breach of a condition in the form *"no development shall be carried out until..."* will not be sufficient to amount to **lawful** (our emphasis) implementation of a planning permission, see *Clwyd CC v. Secretary of State [1982] JPL 696* per Forbes J at 699 (upheld in the Court of Appeal on other grounds at [1983] JPL 50) and *Etheridge v. Secretary of State [1984] JPL 340* per Woolf J at 343. *Etheridge* was expressly endorsed by the Court of Appeal in *Oakimber v Elmbridge Borough Council [1992] JPL 48.*

The classic statement of the principle in the above cases comes from another Court of Appeal case, *FG Whitley v. Secretary of State [1992] 3 PLR 72*. The statement in that case is in fact so classic that it has come to lend its name to the principle (although as we shall see the case itself represents an exception to that principle).

In *Whitley*, the facts were as follows. Permission had been granted in 1973 for the extraction of minerals subject to a number of conditions. Conditions 2, 3 and 4 in effect provided that no working should take place except in accordance with a scheme to be agreed with the local planning authority or, failing agreement, as should be determined by the Secretary of State. Condition 11 stated: "The development hereby permitted shall be begun on or before 30.11.78"

The developers applied 16 months before the deadline for approval of a scheme but the planning authority took no decision until 26 October 1978 when they refused approval. The developers appealed.

The Secretary of State did not give his decision before 30 November 1978, which was the deadline under the permission. In fact, he did not finally issue his decision until 1982. But when he did, he approved a scheme which did not materially differ from the one which had been submitted in 1977.

The developers, anxious not to lose their permission, had meanwhile, prior to approval of the scheme, carried out mining operations (ie pre-approval operations) between 28 November and 8 December 1978. Although it could have done so, the authority served no enforcement notice in respect of those operations – understandable since there was an appeal pending in which the Secretary of State would decide whether or not the scheme was acceptable and since the mining operations had ceased after a few days simply to keep the old mining permission alive if possible.

After the Secretary of State had approved the scheme in 1982 the developers resumed mineral operations (ie post-approval operations) in accordance with the scheme. Then in December 1983, the planning authority served an enforcement notice in respect of the post-approval operations. The developers appealed to the Secretary of State who dismissed their appeal. There was then a further appeal to the High Court and a further appeal to the Court of Appeal. The Court of Appeal held that the developer's appeal to the Secretary of State should have been allowed and that the enforcement notice should be quashed.

Woolf LJ said this at 80B-E:

> *"it is only necessary to ask the single question: are the operations (in other situations the question would refer to the development) permitted by the planning permission read together with its conditions. If the operations contravene the conditions they cannot be properly described as commencing the development authorised by the permission. If they do not comply with the permission they*

> *constitute a breach of planning control and for planning purposes will be unauthorised and thus unlawful. This is the principle which has now been clearly established by the authorities. It is a principle which I would have thought made good sense since I can not conceive that when section 41(1) of the 1971 Act made the planning permission subject to a condition requiring the development to be begun by a specified date, it could have been referring to development other than that which is authorised by the permission... The mining operations to which the planning permission relates are those authorised by the planning permission, not those which are unauthorised, because they contravene conditions contained in the planning permission."*

Applying that principle, the Court of Appeal held that "operations" were permitted by the planning permission read together with the conditions" even though the Secretary of State's approval had come after the commencement of the development. This is why Whitley is in fact an exception to the principle to which it lends its name.

As discussed further below, there is an important difference between "conditions precedent" properly so-called and those which merely require something to be done, such as perhaps the submission of a landscaping scheme, before development commences.

The former are the strict *Whitley* form of condition such as: "no development shall take place before a scheme of working has been submitted to and approved by the local planning authority". An example of the latter might be a condition in the form: "details for the boundary treatment of the site shall be submitted to and approved by the local planning authority before the development commences". As we shall see, however, even conditions in the former, strict *Whitley* form may be construed as not rendering unlawful development commenced in breach of their requirements.

The notable, if not historic, decision heralding the adoption by the courts of a "broad approach" to the application of the Whitley principle is the decision of Sullivan J, as he then was, in *R (Hart Aggregates Ltd) v. Hartlepool BC [2005] JPL 1602.*

In *Hart Aggregates*, the condition in question (condition 10) was said by the planning authority to require that a scheme of restoration had to be agreed with the authority before minerals extraction permitted under the relevant permission commenced and that extraction undertaken without securing that advance approval was not effective to achieve lawful implementation of the permission.

Condition 10 stated: "the worked out areas shall be progressively backfilled and the areas restored to levels shown on the submitted plan or to a level to be agreed with the local planning authority… before extraction is commenced". Extraction commenced in 1971 without the restoration scheme being agreed in advance, but a plan showing restoration levels had been submitted before extraction began.

A subsequent permission was granted in 1989 for an extension to the original extraction area, subject to a condition requiring progressive restoration of both the original and extended area of mineral working. A further subsequent permission was granted under section 73 of the 1990 Act in 1996 for a variation of one of the conditions to which the 1989 permission was subject, and again required progressive restoration of the whole mineral working. Extraction of minerals was carried on continuously form 1971 to the present day.

Also in 1996, the planning authority notified Harts that their quarry was included in the "first list" of mineral sites in the area, pursuant to paras. 3 and 8 of Schedule 13 to the Environment Act 1995. The company subsequently applied for a determination of new conditions under para. 9 of Schedule 13 to the 1995 Act in respect of the 1971 permission. But the authority declined to determine the application on the basis that the 1971 permission had lapsed and so they had no power to consider the application.

Sullivan J nevertheless upheld the company's application for judicial review. He did so both on the narrow basis that condition 10 could properly be construed as not being breached if backfilled areas were restored to levels shown on the plan which had been submitted in 1971 (ie on its face it required that "the worked out areas shall be progressively backfilled and the areas restored to levels shown on the submitted plan <u>or</u> to a level to be agreed with the local planning authority… before extraction is commenced") and on the basis (albeit obiter – ie not forming part of his decisive reasoning) that condition 10 could not properly be construed as a Whitley-form "condition precedent" such that non-compliance with its terms would render implementation of the 1971 permission unlawful.

The judge pointed out that the wording of the condition could be distinguished from that in *Whitley* [1992] which stated in terms that "no extraction shall take place except in accordance with a scheme to be agreed… before extraction takes place". He observed, see para. 58:

> *"Going back to first principles, the starting point should be the proposition that there is no scope for implied conditions in a planning permission. If a local planning authority wishes to impose any obligation upon an applicant by way of a requirement or prohibition, it should do so in express terms, because failure to comply with the condition may, ultimately, lead to prosecution for failure to comply with a breach of condition notice and/or an enforcement notice… The need for a local planning authority to spell out any requirement or prohibition in clear terms applies with particular force where the condition is said to prevent not merely some detail of the development, but the commencement of any development pursuant to the planning permission".*

The judge drew a distinction between conditions precedent which went "to the heart of the permission" and those merely requiring something to be done before development commences.

However, the judge also held that even if he had concluded that condition 10 of the 1971 permission was a "condition precedent" of a kind to which the *Whitley* principle applied, he would nevertheless have concluded that there had been an effective implementation of the 1971 permission, see para. 90:

> *"on the basis that, limestone having been extracted from the original quarry for some 34 years and the restoration scheme mentioned in condition 10 having been overtaken by the restoration provisions in the 1989 and 1996 permissions, it would be both irrational and an abuse of power for the defendant now to commence enforcement action for the purpose of preventing or controlling extraction in the original quarry under the guise of a complaint that the claimants had, many years ago, failed to comply with condition 10, not least because if what is wanted is an up-to-date restoration scheme, that can be obtained by the defendant in its response to the claimant's ROMP application".*

The decision therefore marks a significant revision of what Sullivan J described as the "judge-made" rule about the operation of conditions precedent.

Hart Aggregates was revisited and analysed by HHJ Waksman QC in *Bedford BC v. Secretary of State [2008] EWHC 2304 (Admin).* It will appear that he expresses no reservations about the decision in *Hart Aggregates* and it is notable that, while *Hart* has been mentioned a number of times since it was decided both in the High Court and Court of Appeal, it has not been doubted, see eg *Brent LBC v. Secretary of State [2009] EWCA Civ 328* and *Rastrum Ltd v. Secretary of State [2009] EWCA Civ 1340.*

In *Bedford BC*, HHJ Waksman QC set out a number of questions to be posed in determining whether a development has been lawfully commenced or not. He identified a three-stage process of investigation which the decision maker should go through as follows (see para. 24 of *Bedford BC*):

(1) has there been a breach of condition?

(2) if so, is the effect of that breach of condition such as to render the development as a whole unlawful? (ie has the *Whitley* principle been truly engaged?);

(3) if so, do any of the exceptions to the *Whitley* principle apply (such as irrationality, abuse of power on the part of the planning authority if it sought to enforce, or compliance in substance?).

In most cases, the contentious debates will arise at stages 2 and 3. HHJ Waksman QC goes on to summarise the Stage 2 process in *Bedford BC* at para 35:

> *"A distinction must be drawn for stage 2 purposes between (a) a condition which in truth merely stipulates that something must be done before the time when the development commences, and (b) a condition which in truth goes further and stipulates that the development cannot commence unless the condition is fulfilled … The Whitley principle is only engaged where there is a breach of a class (b) condition."*

An important factor (although subject to what we go on to say below) in making the decision as to whether a condition falls into the class (a) pre-commencement condition category or class (b) condition precedent category appears from the authorities to be its wording. Should the local planning authority wish to prohibit the commencement of any development before a condition is complied with, this must be in "express terms" (see Hart at para 58).

The following examples of wording which signifies a true or "pure" condition precedent are cited in *Bedford BC* at para 35(4):

> *"No extraction shall take place except in accordance with a restoration scheme to be agreed…" (from Hart at para 59); or*
>
> *"No works shall be commenced on site until … fencing approved by the local planning authority … shall have been erected…" (Condition 8 in Leisure Great Britain v. Isle of Wight Council (2000) 80 P & CR 370, cited in Bedford BC at para 11); or*
>
> *"The development shall not commence until the exchange land described in article 30 of the Order has been made suitable for use as open space by…" (Condition 21 in Hammerton v London Underground Ltd [2002] EWHC 2307 (Admin) 133, cited in Bedford BC at para 15).*

That the interpretation of the wording may be significant in deciding the scope of a condition is emphasised in *Bedford BC* at para 35(4): *"Provided that it is made clear enough in the condition that the development's commencement itself is truly conditional upon the fulfilment of the condition, the subject matter of the condition need not be central; i.e. not concern itself directly with the activity permitted, for example, the extraction or the building".*

This latter statement might be taken as suggesting that the wording of the condition is irrevocably determinative of the question whether it is a "pure" condition precedent. However, there must remain other factors to be taken into account. Sullivan J said this in *Hart* at para 67:

> *"Each case will have to be considered upon its own particular facts, and the outcome may well depend upon the number and the significance of the conditions that have not been complied with."*

See also what is said in *Bedford BC* at para 49:

> *"In paragraphs 29 and 30 the inspector does invoke "the heart of permission" dicta of Sullivan J. I see nothing wrong in this. In truth it is a matter of analysis, and can easily be gleaned from the words of the conditions themselves and the stated reasons for imposing them. It seems obvious that landscaping is not central to the conversion of the Barn and boundaries equally so, if the landowner should choose to have boundary treatments. Moreover, they are not separate works which of necessity must be done or approved before building can sensibly start."*

Nevertheless, since the conditions in question in *Bedford BC* were in the following "pre-commencement" condition form, it remains the position there has as yet been no case law authority that has dealt with a situation involving a departure from the interpretation indicated by "pure" condition precedent prohibitory wording. The conditions in *Bedford* were as follows:

> *"Before the development is commenced a landscaping scheme to include all hard surfaces and earth mounding shall be submitted for approval by the District Planning Authority, and all planting thereby approved shall be carried out to their satisfaction by a date not later than the end of the full planting season immediately following the completion of that development"*

and

> *"Details of all boundary treatments are to be submitted to and approved by the District Planning Authority, prior to the commencement of development."*

See also Greyfort *Properties v. Secretary of State [2011] EWCA Civ 908* in which development commenced without complying with a condition requiring that "before any work is commenced on the site the ground floor levels of the building hereby permitted shall be agreed with the Local Planning Authority in writing" was held to be unlawful.

There is a yet further point which emerges from *Whitley*, *Hart Aggregates* and *Greyfort* which is that the effectiveness of implementation of a planning permission can be judged in the light of the expediency of taking enforcement action. For example, where the work relied on was started in breach of condition, but the approvals were obtained within the lifetime of the permission, enforcement proceedings would be too technical. Where works contravened a blanket prohibition but were not themselves something to which the missing approvals could relate, or where the works in breach were of no planning significance, the position had similarly to be to be judged in the light of enforcement proceedings, see *Hart* at [80] citing Ouseley J's discussion of Whitley in *Hammerton v. London Underground Ltd* [2002] EWHC 2307 (Admin) 133, subsequently endorsed in *R (Prokopp) v London Underground Ltd* [2003] EWCA Civ 961 per Buxton LJ at [85].

In any event, it is to be borne in mind that the decision in *Hart Aggregates* was also made on the yet further alternative (and therefore also obiter) basis that after the lapse of 34 years "it would be both irrational and an abuse of power for the defendant now to commence enforcement action for the purpose of preventing or controlling extraction in the original quarry under the guise of a complaint that the claimants had, many years ago, failed to comply with condition 10", see again para. 90 of Sullivan J's judgment. This can be compared with what HHJ Waksman said in *Bedford* at para. 24 about the considerations to address at Stage 3 of his analysis, namely, whether any of the exceptions to the *Whitley* principle apply, such as irrationality, abuse of power on the part of the planning authority if it sought to enforce, or compliance in substance.

The debate in relation to compliance with conditions characterised as being conditions precedent will therefore continue.

The authors were involved in a case where an Inspector was prepared to find that the following conditions were not conditions precedent going to the heart of the permission concerned which may be of use in considering the approach of the Planning Inspectorate to the issues arising. The Inspector held as follows;

> *"The 1996 planning permission was subject to a number of 'conditions precedent', in that they required certain details of the development to be submitted to and approved in writing by the local planning authority before the development commenced.*
>
> *Two of the leading cases on 'conditions precedent' are F G Whitley & Sons v SSW and Clwyd CC [1992] JPL 856 (Court of Appeal) and R (Hart Aggregates Ltd) v Hartlepool BC [2005] EWCA 840 (Admin).*
>
> *Condition No. 9 was a landscaping condition of the type identified in Whitley, being a condition precedent that normally prevents lawful commencement of development until it is discharged within the life of the permission.*
>
> *[Cond 9: "no development shall take place until there has been submitted to and approved by the local planning authority a scheme of landscaping…"]*
>
> *In Whitley the Court of Appeal held that the only question to be asked was whether the development was permitted by the planning permission read together with its conditions. If the development contravenes the conditions it cannot be properly described as*

commencing the development authorised by the permission. The Court held in this particular case that once the scheme had been approved the works were no longer enforceable against and the development had been validly commenced. The Courts have, in subsequent cases, been prepared to apply the Whitley principle flexibly, recognising that in extensive developments there may need to be some latitude given in terms of timing provided there was no prejudice to the purpose of the conditions. These later judgments indicate that all circumstances of the case must be considered in a fair and commonsense manner.

Condition Nos. 2 and 6 require works to be carried out before the use commences. These are conditions of the type identified in Hart Aggregates.

[Cond 2: "Before the use is commenced, the access from the existing highway shall be laid out and constructed to the satisfaction of the Local Planning Authority after consultation with the Local Highway Authority"

Cond 6: "The permanent space to be reserved on the site for turning and parking shall be provided before the use commences and thereafter maintained"]

In Hart Aggregates the Court held that a distinction had to be drawn between a condition which requires some action to be undertaken before development is commenced and a condition which expressly prohibits any development taking place before a particular requirement has been met. Sullivan J. took the view that even so it is necessary for the condition both to be expressly prohibitive of commencement of development and to go to the heart of the permission. Only when both tests are satisfied is it a condition precedent to which the Whitley principle applies and where the development would be development without planning permission.

From the cases it follows that failure to satisfy a condition requiring approval of some detail of the development "before development commences" (such as Condition Nos. 2 and 6) would not be likely to render the whole development unlawful as it would not be an express prohibition.

A condition that required "that no development should take place before ... " (such as Condition No.9) would be expressly prohibitive, but on the Sullivan J analysis if it did not concern something that went to the heart of the permission (for example, a landscaping condition) it would not render the whole development unlawful.

In the light of these judgments, and the particular circumstances of the 1996 planning permission, I consider that this planning permission was implemented and the development was lawful".

Summary

This chapter has been concerned with the basics of certificates and sets out the basic requirements as to what has to be proven and deals with some peripheral issues and interaction with other parts of the development control system. The questions in the checklist are designed to assist with asking all the right questions to first of all decide if an application might be made and to consider other relevant issues.

CHECKLIST

1. What form of development is involved?

2. Is it operational development?

3. Is it a change of use?

4. Is it a combination of the two?

5. Is there an enforcement notice on the land?

6. Is it in force?

7. What are the requirements and how does this relate to the proposed claim for immunity?

8. If concerned with a condition what are the actual requirements and has there been a breach?

9. If there are pre-commencement conditions are either the *Whitley* or *Hart Aggregates* principles engaged?

10. Was the condition properly imposed in the first place?

CHAPTER TWO

TIME LIMITS

This chapter is divided into two distinct sections following the changes introduced by the Levelling Up and Regeneration Act 2023 which in essence no longer discriminates between the different types of breach and provides a 10-year immunity period for all breaches of planning control that occur after 25th April 2023. It should be noted that the changes apply to England only and the "old" time limits still apply in Wales.

The authors, in common with other commentators, have wondered why such a change was required as it seems to them that if a building has been in existence for more than 4 years without objection then the need for enforcement action must be called into question and we wonder how the expediency test can be met.

There are transitional provisions that will need to be taken into account as well which we discuss later in this chapter.

The "Old" Regime

These are still important as breaches of planning control that had become immune from enforcement action or that had occurred prior to 25th April 2024 but had not yet become immune will be subject to the rules that had applied up to that date.

There are three main time limits that we are concerned with and these are set out in section 171 B. These are the same as for the time limits for taking enforcement action. However, there is a potential interaction between some of the time limits that we will now examine.

It is an important point to note that time cannot run so that immunity accrues if there are gaps in the continuity of the use following its initial commencement, see *Secretary of State v. Thurrock BC [2002] 2 PLR 43, CA.*

The *Thurrock* case involved a change of use to airfield use in 1981 but "the degree of activity fluctuated" subsequently, see para. 3. It was held that the Inspector made an error by considering the commencement of flying activity as establishing lawful use rights which could only be lost by abandonment, see para. 15(vi). The court further held that

> *"If at any time during the relevant [10 year] period the LPA would not have been able to take enforcement proceedings in respect of the breach, for example, because no breach was taking place, then any such period cannot count towards the rolling period of years which gives rise to the immunity"*, see para. 15(iv).

The court nevertheless accepted that there could be "fallow periods" before the expiry of the ten-year period when nothing objectionable was going on on the land (because, for instance, activities ceased overnight, over weekends or for a break in the summer or because the activities carried on were seasonal) which would not prevent time running so as to count towards the full ten years, see para. 18. This was to be distinguished from the situation where a use had permanently ceased before immunity accrued (so there would have been no activity going on which could have been enforced against), see para. 28.

Swale BC v. Secretary of State [2006] JPL 886, CA, is in similar vein. In that case, the Inspector applied the wrong test when considering whether lawful use rights had accrued in respect of the landowner's occupation of a barn for residential purposes by referring to "substantial periods" when the barn was occupied, rather than acknowledging that that implied that there were also "substantial periods" when it was not occupied, and having himself referred to an "erratic pattern of use" over the 4 year period which was relevant in that case, see para. 28. That is, lawful use rights were not secured because of interruptions to the continuity of that use which would otherwise have resulted in the accrual of immunity.

The above is an aspect which applicants and authorities need to keep firmly in mind when calculating the running of the time period over which it is contended that immunity has accrued.

Operational Development

As with enforcement cases the applicable time limit is 4 years from the date of completion of the relevant development. Section 171 B (1) refers to "the carrying out without planning permission of building, engineering, mining or other operations in, on, over or under land…." thus mirroring the definition of development in section 55(1). What constitutes completion will need to be ascertained. The case of *Sage v Secretary of State for Environment, Transport and the Regions [2001] EWCA Civ 1100* established that this means looking at what works will actually require permission and which would constitute a breach of planning control if they were carried out. Thus, works which comprise internal works only or which would be Permitted Development would not be a breach of planning control. This means that, for example, if someone were to construct a dwellinghouse without planning permission it would be regarded as complete for enforcement purposes a soon as all of the external works were completed. That does not automatically mean that the use will also be immune as we shall see shortly.

Difficulties can arise in practice where development is undertaken in apparent breach of condition. The most obvious example would be where there are various pre-commencement conditions attached to the permission which have not been discharged. Assuming these are what we might call Hart Aggregates conditions as discussed previously then in the circumstances now described any application could only be based on the fact that the actual development had been undertaken as unauthorised operational development rather than development in breach of condition. The implications of such a position could be quite profound. For example, if the development were say a large housing estate and it was built without the necessary conditions having been discharged prior to commencement or dealt with in accordance with the principles in Henry Boot the issue of whether or not the requirements of the section 106 agreement have been engaged must be at the forefront of any considerations. If payments had actually been made it must be at the very least arguable that they were made under a mistake of fact and should be returned. This is because section 106 agreements invariably have a provision which provides that the requirements are only triggered by among other things implementation of the permission. If the permission has never been implemented then the requirements are never triggered.

It is not beyond the realms of possibility that there are many large estates up and down the country where such a situation has occurred given the previous laissez faire approach of local authorities and developers to pre-commencement conditions. Due diligence as part of the conveyancing process has not always been as thorough as might expose such a situation. Apart from the issue of whether or not section 106 obligations have been wrongly performed there will be numerous houses with at best a questionable planning status and at worst mortgages will have been granted on the basis that the property can be used for residential purposes. We are not seeking to trigger either a plethora of litigation claims or applications for certificates of lawfulness as letting sleeping dogs lie may be the best response but there may be cases where it will be necessary to clarify the planning status of properties and it may be that an application for a certificate of lawfulness will be the only sensible way to resolve the issue.

Change of Use

There are two different time limits involved here. The first time period which concerns dwellinghouses is 4 years from the change of use occurring. Section 171B (2) refers to "the change of use of any building to use as a single dwellinghouse". Applying the definition in section 336 the "building" will include "part of a building" resulting in a position where the subdivision of an existing dwellinghouse into two or more dwellinghouses would be covered by the provisions of this section. This is again in line with section 55 (3).

A different situation arose in the case of *Arun District Council v Brown [2006] EWCA Civ 1172.* In that case permission had been granted for a granny annex subject to the normal condition requiring that it be used in conjunction with the dwelling house to which it related. In due course the annex was let to students. The council took enforcement action basing its decision on the fact that there had not been a breach for 10 years and thus the condition was still capable of enforcement. The case eventually came before the Court of Appeal which decided that the time limit for enforcement action in respect of a change of use of any building to a single dwellinghouse was 4 years regardless of whether the breach of planning control consisted of development without permission or breach of a condition of planning permission. The *Arun* case was considered by the Supreme Court in the *Welywyn Hatfield* case which we will deal with in a moment and was distinguished but not overruled and thus remains good law. Lord Mance thought that the court of Appeal's approach gave subsection (2) "a generous interpretation" but did not disapprove of such generosity.

It is an important point to note that time cannot run so that immunity accrues if there are gaps in the continuity of the use following its initial commencement, see *Secretary of State v Thurrock BC [2002] 2 PLR 43, CA.*

The *Thurrock* case involved a change of use to airfield use in 1981 but "the degree of activity fluctuated" subsequently, see para 3 of the judgment. It was held that the Inspector made an error by considering the commencement of flying activity as establishing lawful use rights which could only be lost by abandonment, see para 15(vi)of the judgment. The court further held that;

> *"If at any time during the relevant [10 year] period the LPA would not have been able to take enforcement proceedings in respect of the breach, for example, because no breach was taking place, then any such period cannot count towards the rolling period of years which gives rise to immunity"*, see para 15 (iv).

Schiemann LJ qualified this by saying at para. 28 of *Thurrock* that;

> *"I accept Mr Corner's point that an enforcement notice can lawfully be issued notwithstanding that at the moment of issue the activity objected to is not going on – because it is the week-end or the factory's summer holiday, for instance. The land would still be properly described as being used for the objectionable activity. However, I would reject Mr Hockman's submission that enforcement action can be taken once the new activity which resulted from the material change in the use of land has permanently ceased. I accept that there will be borderline cases when it is not clear whether the land is being used for the objectionable activity. These are matters of judgment for others".*

Chadwick LJ made the further point that, on the other hand, it would be a "nonsense" to suggest that an enforcement notice might be served in respect of a "sleeping use" which was "notionally continuing" even though it had ceased to be an active use before lawful use right could have accrued, see para. 58.

Swale BC v Secretary of State [2006] JPL 886, CA is in similar vein. In that case, the Inspector applied the wrong test when considering whether lawful use rights had accrued in respect of the landowner's occupation of a barn for residential purposes by referring to "substantial periods" when the barn was occupied, rather than acknowledging that there were also "substantial periods" when it was not occupied, and having himself referred to an "erratic pattern of use" over the 4 year period which was relevant in that case, see para 28 of the judgment. That is, lawful rights were not secured because of interruptions to the continuity of that use which would otherwise have resulted in the accrual of immunity.

The above is an aspect that applicants and authorities need to keep firmly in mind when calculating the running of the time period over which it is contended that immunity had accrued.

The second time period is 10 years and covers "any other breach of planning control" as specified in section 171B (3). The straightforward application of this subsection would be for all changes of use involving non-residential changes of use but as well shall see there is an exception to that basic proposition. The 10-year time limit also applies to breaches of condition, as being "[an]other breach of planning control" and we consider this under a separate heading below.

A further issue arises between the interaction of the time period for operational development and the use of the land on which the unauthorised development has occurred. In the case of *Sumner v Secretary of State for Communities and Local Government [2010] EWHC 372 (Admin)* it was argued that where a building had become immune from enforcement action then the use of the building should be regarded as lawful in the same way as a planning permission. This proposition was rejected by the court which held that the use could not be regarded as lawful just because the time period for taking enforcement action had expired. A situation can thus arise where a local planning authority cannot take action to require removal of a building but because the use of the building has not been for more than 10 years then technically an enforcement notice could be served to prevent its continued use. This outcome was considered by Lord Mance in the *Welwyn Hatfied* case. In paragraph 17 of his judgment he discusses this situation and concludes that "once a planning authority has allowed the four year period for enforcement against the building to pass, principles of fairness and good governance could, in appropriate cases, preclude it from subsequently taking enforcement steps to render the building useless." He did not elaborate as to what an appropriate case might be but there is sufficient comfort in the judgment whereby those who are in a situation where continued occupation of a dwelling could be an issue can point to paragraph 17 if confronted with potential enforcement action by a local planning authority.

The authors' instinct on this aspect has been held to be correct, see the recent case of *Secretary of State for Levelling Up, Housing and Communities v Caldwell [2024] EWCA Civ 467 in which the Court of Appeal held (at para. 45)* that;

> *"The construction, without planning permission, of a new dwelling house on an undeveloped site, as took place here, was operational development to which the four-year time limit under section 171B(1) applied, not the ten-year time limit for material changes of use under section 171B(3) . Otherwise, section 171B(1) would have become obsolete, or largely so. Building a dwelling house on land previously undeveloped will, of course, be likely to result in a change of use of that land. But this does not mean that there was a ten-year time limit for enforcement against such operational development, when the statutory time limit for enforcing against unauthorised operational development was four years under section 171B(1) . That was not the effect of the principle in Murfitt v*

Secretary of State for the Environment and East Cambridgeshire DC (1980) 40 P. & C.R. 254"

This now takes us on to the *Welwyn Hatfield* case. This case came before the Supreme court and is reported as *Welwyn Hatfield Borough Council v Secretary of State for communities and Local Government & ANOR [2011] UKSC 15*. The facts are straightforward. Planning permission was granted for a barn. The landowner actually constructed a dwelling hidden behind straw bales and after he had occupied it for 4 years applied for a certificate of lawfulness arguing that he had changed the use from the barn even though the building was never constructed as a barn and was never actually used a such. The Supreme Court overturned the Court of Appeal and held that there was no such thing as a change of use from a "no use" to use a single dwellinghouse. The building that had been constructed could not be regarded as having any permitted use as it was unlawful and not in accordance with the permission for the barn. The relevant time period was therefore 10 years in respect of the use and not 4 as subsection (2) of section 171B did not apply.

The *Welwyn Hatfield* case also dealt with a further point relating to dishonesty. The landowner had made various positive and deliberately misleading statements to the council. The Supreme Court made it clear that in these circumstances it would not countenance a situation where the landowner would be permitted to profit directly from that deception.

This issue has now been put on a statutory footing with the insertion of sections 171BA, BB and BC. These provisions to which section 171 B is specifically subject enable a local authority to apply for what is called a planning enforcement order to a magistrates' court and, if granted, the council can then issue an enforcement notice within 12 months of the order being granted. The effect of these provisions on time limits is carried through to section 191(3A) which provides;

> *"In determining for the purposes of this section whether the time for taking enforcement action in respect of a matter has expired, that time is to be taken not to have expired if—*
>
> *(a) the time for applying for an order under section 171BA(1) (a "planning enforcement order") in relation to the matter has not expired,*
>
> *(b) an application has been made for a planning enforcement order in relation to the matter and the application has neither been decided nor been withdrawn, or*
>
> *(c) a planning enforcement order has been made in relation to the matter, the order has not been rescinded and the enforcement year for the order (whether or not it has begun) has not expired".*

The council must apply for a planning enforcement order within 6 months of the date "on which evidence of the apparent breach of planning control sufficient in the opinion of the authority to justify the application came to the authority's knowledge." No doubt there will be litigation as to what knowledge will suffice for the purpose of an application and how that knowledge would be acquired. For example, would an application for building regulation approval constitute sufficient evidence? This will be relevant to an application for a certificate of lawfulness but even then that may not be the full answer.

When an application is made the magistrates can only make an order if the two conditions in section 171BC (1) are met. These are;

> *"(a) the court is satisfied, on the balance of probabilities, that the apparent breach, or any of the matters constituting the apparent breach, has (to any extent) been deliberately concealed by any person or persons, and*

(b) *the court considers it just to make the order having regard to all the circumstances"*

There would appear to be some scope to seek to persuade a court that it was not just to make an order but if there was some form of concealment this may be more difficult. It might be that if the concealment had been done by a third party then it might be easier to persuade the court if the current owner had not been guilty of seeking to hide or conceal the breach.

These provisions were the subject of judicial scrutiny in the case of *Jackson v Secretary of State for communities and Local Government [2015] EWHC 20 (Admin).* In that case an argument was put forward to the effect that the new provisions had been enacted in order to replace the decision in *Welwyn Hatfield* and thus any issues concerning concealment etc had to be dealt with in accordance with those provisions. That approach was rejected with the court confirming that the *Welwyn* principles would still apply as the statutory provisions could not be seen as a complete replacement as they only dealt with deliberate concealment and did not deal with any of the other matters such as "bribery, coercion or menaces" that would engage the principles in *Welwyn Hatfield.*

Breaches of Condition

As noted above, the relevant time limit where breaches of condition are concerned is 10 years, the same as for non-residential changes of use. As for changes of use in breach of planning control, see *Secretary of State v. Thurrock BC [2002] JPL 1278*, the breach must have been continuous over the period of 10 years, see *Nicholson v. Secretary of State [1998] 2 P.L.R. 6.*

In *Nicholson*, it is to be noted that the breach (of an agricultural occupancy condition) was not continuing at the date of the application and the court further held that any recommencement of use in breach of the condition would give rise to a fresh breach. So on the basis of the decision in *Nicholson*, the breach had to be continuous and had to be subsisting at the time of the application.

Nicholson was subsequently applied in *Ellis v Secretary of State [2010] 1 P & CR 21*. The Court stated that Parliament was concerned with conferring immunity on a particular failure to comply with a condition and not on a type of failure generally.

It is to be noted that *Nicholson* and *Ellis* expressly state that, in such breach of agricultural occupancy condition cases where there is a "continuing requirement for commitment" as contrasted with conditions containing a mere "once and for all requirement", the breach which is contended to be immune must be subsisting at the date of the application. Thus, in *Ellis*, no immunity accrued even though the dwelling in question had been occupied without complying with the agricultural occupancy condition to which it was subject from 1961 to 2000 since the relevant breach had ceased and so time would start to run again on re-commencement of non-compliant occupation.

The authors always regarded this line of case law as inconsistent with the general principle that immunity should accrue after the relevant "limitation" period in section 171B has elapsed, compare *Thurrock* above and note also that *Panton and Farmer v Secretary of State [1191] 1 PLR 92* states that once immunity from enforcement in a change of use case has been established (by the running of time counted from the date of the breach) that immunity can only be lost subsequently through abandonment, the formation of another planning unit or the making of a material change of use.

Once again, the authors' instinct has proved to be correct in that *Nicholson* and *Ellis* were expressly not followed in R (Ocado Retail Ltd) v Islington London Borough Council [2021] P.T.S.R. 183, see per Holgate J (as he then was) at para. 159;

> *"I have reached the clear and certain conclusion that, with great respect, I should not follow the decisions in Ellis and in Nicholson, that a breach of condition which has become lawful after continuing for ten years does not remain lawful unless that breach continues thereafter. I do not consider that those decisions can be reconciled with the following key points, along with the earlier analysis in this judgment:*
>
> *(i) The requirement that a breach should continue during the immunity period is not contained in the legislation (Sullivan J in R (North Devon District Council) v First Secretary of State [2004] JPL 1396, at para 30).*
>
> *(ii) That requirement is based solely on the rationale for the time limits in section 171B, namely that throughout the relevant period the local planning authority had the opportunity to take enforcement action but failed to do so. The continuity requirement is only concerned with whether the time period for satisfying an immunity period is running. Time only runs while a breach of planning control, whether a change of use or a breach of condition, is liable to enforcement action. Time does not run when a use or breach of condition has ceased.*
>
> *(iii) Once an immunity period is satisfied, the legislation prohibits the taking of enforcement action thereafter (section 171B). It follows that from then on, any question about whether there is an ongoing breach of planning control against which a local planning authority would be able to take enforcement action would be completely irrelevant. The raison d'être for the*

continuity requirement disappears upon the expiration of an immunity period. There is no need to consider whether time is running for the purposes of section 171B.

(iv) Once an immunity period expires, what was formerly a breach of planning control becomes "lawful at any time", save only that that planning right does not accrue if it would contravene the requirements of an enforcement notice then in force.

(v) There is nothing in the legislation to indicate that the requirement for continuity to satisfy an immunity period also characterises the nature of the legal right which accrues upon the expiration of a time limit in section 171B, or conditions the basis upon which that right may continue to exist thereafter, or that a right which accrues under section 191(2) or (3) ceases to exist when it ceases to be exercised.

(vi) The legislation does not treat a use, operation or breach of condition differently in these respects".

Another case on agricultural occupancy conditions is *North Devon DC v. Secretary of State [2004] 3 PLR 62* in which the asserted breach was use for holiday lettings in summer months. That was held not to be sufficient to amount to occupation of the property in breach of condition (i.e. by someone not employed or mainly employed in agriculture) for a continuous period of ten years ending with the application.

The 1998 *North Devon* case is to be distinguished from *North Devon v Secretary of State [2004] 3 PLR 62*. In that case, by contrast, a property subject to a seasonal occupancy condition had been occupied full time over ten years. The court rejected the submission that a "fresh breach" occurred at the end of each seasonal period when occupation continued over the winter. The Court, Sullivan J, rejected a "mechanistic" application of the approach in *Nicholson*.

As noted above, *Arun DC v Secretary of State [2006] EWCA Civ 1172* is a case involving a breach of condition requiring that an extension to an existing house (for use as a granny annexe) should not be occupied as a separate unit of accommodation which was then separately occupied by students. That was nevertheless held to benefit from the provision in section 172B(2) relating to changes of use to a use as a single dwelling house.

The "New" Rules

Section 171 of the 1990 Act was amended by the Levelling Up and Regeneration Act 2023 as follows;

> *Enforcement of planning controls*
>
> ***115 Time limits for enforcement***
>
> *(1) In section 171B of TCPA 1990 (time limits), in subsection (1), for the words from "four years" to the end substitute—*
>
> > *(a) in the case of a breach of planning control in England, ten years beginning with the date on which the operations were substantially completed, and*
> >
> > *(b) in the case of a breach of planning control in Wales, four years beginning with the date on which the operations were substantially completed."*
>
> *(2) In that section, in subsection (2), for the words from "four years" to the end substitute—*

> *(a) in the case of a breach of planning control in England, ten years beginning with the date of the breach, and*
>
> *(b) in the case of a breach of planning control in Wales, four years beginning with the date of the breach."*

Section 115 was brought into force by the *The Planning Act 2008 (Commencement No. 8) and Levelling-up and Regeneration Act 2023 (Commencement No. 4 and Transitional Provisions) Regulations 2024.*

Regulation 5 of those regulations provide the transitional provisions as follows;

> *Transitional provision: time limits for enforcement*
>
> *5. The amendments made to the 1990 Act by section 115 of the 2023 Act (time limits for enforcement) do not apply where—*
>
> *(a) in respect of a breach of planning control referred to in section 171B(1) of the 1990 Act (5) (time limits), the operations were substantially completed, or*
>
> *(b) in respect of a breach of planning control referred to in section 171B(2) of the 1990 Act (time limits), the breach occurred,*
>
> *before the day on which that section comes into force.*

The authors had formed a view prior to the new provisions coming into force that there was potential for litigation in respect of those breaches of planning control that had become immune from enforcement action prior to the new provision coming into effect. This is due to the effect of section 191(2) of the 1990 Act which provides that "*uses and operations are lawful*" following the expiry if the relevant period for acquiring immunity. Thus, the argument would have been that the new provisions could not prevent the issue of a Certificate in circumstances where the use or operations had become lawful prior to those new provisions coming into effect.

However, the transitional provisions ensure that such litigation should not be necessary as they ensure that pre-existing breaches continue to enjoy exemption from the new provisions. It is important to, therefore, bear in mind that it is only breaches of planning control that have occurred after 25th April 2024 that will be subject to the new time limits and provided the evidence is sufficiently clear any breach that has commenced prior to that date can still obtain a Certificate if all t ether requirements for such issue are met

Summary

This chapter has been concerned with the issue of time limits. As with most things pertaining to the planning system what might at first glance appear straightforward is nothing of the sort and there is now a plethora of potential time periods and other considerations that will have to be tackled. The relevant time limits can be summarized as shown in the table below

Breaches Prior to 25th April 2024 and Wales Post That Date

Form of Development	Relevant Time Limit
Operational development involving construction in, on over or under land	4 years
Change of Use of a building or land	10 years
Subdivision of an existing dwelling into two or more dwellings	4 years
Breach of Condition	10 years
Change of Use of land or building to use as a dwelling	10 years but see comments of Lord Mance at para 17 of Welwyn Hatfield
Breach of condition relating to dwellings and annexes	4 years as per the Arun District Council case

Breaches After 25th April 2024 in England

10 years for all breaches

CHECKLIST

1. Which time limit(s) is engaged? Was it pre or post 25th April 2024? This will involve re-visiting the question as to what form of development has occurred.

2. If a dwelling is involved is it a change of use of an existing building or a subdivision of an existing dwellinghouse?

3. Is there an actual change of use of a building or was it constructed from scratch and first used as a dwelling?

4. Is the building immune but not the use?

5. Has there been dishonesty either by misleading the local authority or by general concealment?

6. Are the statutory provisions engaged? If so, have all the procedural requirements been met? What arguments, if any, exist to seek to persuade the court not to make an order?

CHAPTER THREE

STANDARD AND BURDEN OF PROOF

The planning authority faced with an application for a CLEUD will have to be satisfied as to the weight and reliability of the evidence before it. The now-cancelled Circular 10/97 stated that the onus/burden of proof in an application was "firmly" on the applicant. That phrase is not repeated in the Planning Practice Guidance (PPG) which supersedes the Circular but there is no reason for assuming that the principle does not continue to apply.

As we will see, the standard of proof is the ordinary civil standard of proof "on the balance of probability" NOT the higher criminal standard of proof "beyond reasonable doubt", see para. 17c-006 of the PPG Guidance.

The same paragraph in the Guidance emphasises that the evidence produced by the applicant must be "sufficiently precise and unambiguous" to justify the grant of a certificate.

The Guidance states that the applicant is responsible for providing sufficient information to support an application, but notes that a local planning authority always needs to co-operate with an applicant who is seeking information that the authority may hold about the planning status of the land concerned, see para. 006. It goes on to say that a local planning authority is entitled to canvass evidence from others if it so wishes to do so before determining an application but warns that if the authority obtains any such evidence, it needs to be shared with the applicant to give them the opportunity to comment on it and possibly produce their own counter-evidence, see same paragraph.

This of course is simply to ensure compliance with the principles of natural justice.

Potentially more controversially, the Guidance also says this (again in para. 006):

> *"In the case of applications for existing use, if a local planning authority has no evidence itself, nor any from others, to contradict or otherwise make the applicant's version of events less than probable, there is no good reason to refuse the application, provided the applicant's evidence alone is sufficiently precise and unambiguous to justify the grant of a certificate on the balance of probability".*

We have referred above to the fact that an application for a certificate does not necessarily require corroboration by any independent evidence. In practice, however, it will normally be desirable for the applicant to supplement their own evidence with evidence from others and/or from other documentary sources from the point of view of making the strongest case on their behalf and to ensure that they meet the requisite standard of proof.

But the Guidance in para. 17c-006 might be read as suggesting that the planning authority should simply grant a certificate where they have no evidence in their own possession which contradicts that produced by the applicant. As noted by the editor of the Journal of Planning Law in the case comment on *Gabbitas v. Secretary of State [1985] JPL 630*, authorities should be conscious that "*the temptation on an [applicant] (who is also giving evidence) to emphasise those facts which suit his case will be strong*".

In any event, the above paragraph in the Guidance does remind authorities that, if taken alone, the applicant's evidence must be "sufficiently precise and unambiguous" to justify the grant of a certificate. That is, the absence of a requirement for corroboration does not provide an unimpeded route to the grant of a certificate where the applicant is simply relying on their own say-so.

Summary

This chapter has been concerned with the standard of proof and draws attention to the fact that the relevant standard is the civil rather than the criminal standard of proof that is relevant. We now turn to production of the evidence to meet the standard of proof required.

CHECKLIST

1. Key question: is there sufficient evidence to establish "on the balance of probability" that the development which is the subject of the application is lawful?

2. Does the authority have any evidence of its own to set against that relied on by the applicant?

3. In any event, is the applicant's evidence sufficiently precise and unambiguous to justify the grant of a certificate?

CHAPTER FOUR

FORM AND CONTENT OF APPLICATIONS

The first point to make is that there is not prescribed form although most, if not all local authorities have a standard form that can be accessed via the Planning Portal. Given the tick box mentality that currently pervades all aspects of life an applicant may need to remind admin staff of this at some point if the model form is not used. Having said this the existence of a standard form and its completion will no doubt aid registration and thus early determination of an application.

The basic requirements for a valid application are set out in section 191(5). This includes such matters as the relevant paragraph under which the application is made, the date the breach began, use class (where appropriate), name and address of applicant, interest in the land, a plan and the evidence relied upon. All of the matters are covered in the standard form. Please see comments in relation to CLOPUDs in the chapter concerning them.

The specific formalities for an application under section 191 are set out in Art. 39 of the Development Management Procedure Order 2015. Art. 39(1) requires the applicant to use the application form published by the Secretary of State (or a form substantially to the same effect) and to specify on it the land to which the application relates, describe the use, operations or other matter in question (and include the particulars specified or referred to in the form).

Art. 39(2) further provides:

"(2) An application to which paragraph (1) applies must be accompanied by

(a) a plan identifying the land to which the application relates drawn to an identified scale and showing the direction of North;

(b) such evidence verifying the information included in the application as the applicant can provide; and

(c) a statement setting out the applicant's interest in the land, the name and address of any other person known to the applicant to have an interest in the land and whether any such other person has been notified of the application".

So how does an applicant go about assembling an application? The most relevant issue has to be evidence.

Evidence

They say that information is power. In this context information is vital. Without it there will not be much ability to make any progress. For the purposes of making an application there are two types of evidence that should be considered namely direct evidence and documentary evidence.

Direct Evidence

This is the most important and most often overlooked part of the jigsaw. There is a debate as to how this evidence should be presented and whether or not there is a need for the evidence to be in the form of a statutory declaration. There is no actual requirement for sworn evidence to support an application. However, if one considers that if there is an appeal against a refusal the evidence at that stage will be taken on oath as matters of fact are at issue then evidence in the form of statutory declarations should be the norm. From the authors' perspective if an applicant is prepared to go to the time and expense of having statutory declarations prepared and sworn this adds a certain credibility to the application and puts the evidence on a higher footing than say a simple letter setting out alleged facts. Indeed, the authors would not contemplate submitting an application unless the direct evidence is in sworn form. This is, however, a personal preference and if an applicant does not wish to present an application in this way the local planning authority will have to take a view as to the veracity, or otherwise, of the evidence.

From an applicant's point of view they should try and get more than one declaration. This can include current or ex-employees, neighbours, customers or suppliers or professional advisors. The main requirement is that whoever is to provide a declaration has knowledge over a relevant period that coincides with the period over which it is claimed immunity from enforcement action has been acquired. Each witness does not have to have knowledge over the whole time period provided the totality of the evidence from those providing it covers the relevant time period.

With regard to corroboration the Local Planning Authority may need to be reminded that there is no actual requirement for corroboration. The Court held in *Gabbitas v Newham LB* that there is no need for the applicant's evidence to be corroborated by "independent" evidence for it to be acceptable. Unless there is evidence to contradict the applicant's version or the submitted evidence is not sufficiently precise or unambiguous the submitted evidence should be accepted.

This will sometimes cause difficulty in practice as we are talking about discharging the burden of proof and the weight that is given to the evidence that has been submitted. What can a local authority do when faced with a bold assertion that is not supported by any corroboration or extraneous evidence? In some cases it may not be able to do anything whilst in others a refusal is the only answer. The planning authority will have to make the decision accordingly. We will mention this again when we look at informal discussions in a moment.

From the authors' perspective acting for applicants, they would not contemplate making an application that was not supported by as much supporting evidence as can be produced together with some corroborating statutory declarations if they can be provided.

However, there is no requirement for Statutory Declaration sand whilst the lack of such evidence may be a material factor in deciding weight we do not think the planning authority would find much sympathy with an Inspector if the only reason for refusal was a refusal to reduce a written statement to a Statutory Declaration.

Drafting Statutory Declarations

The authors are sometimes asked to look at applications on behalf of LPA's and in their experience the standard of evidential preparation is sometimes significantly lacking. In order to assist both applicants and local authorities what follows is a simple guide to drafting that the authors provide to clients so that they will know what will be needed to prepare the necessary documentation.

The main points for those who are swearing statutory declarations is to ensure that the following is evident from the sworn document -

- Say who they are
- What interest in the premises, if any, they have

- How long they have known the land or the applicant or the activities

- Describe as precisely as they can how the land was used or the development undertaken

- Try to be as precise as possible including dates where relevant and refer to any exhibits at appropriate points

- If hearsay evidence is included then state the basis of the knowledge or information

- Above all tell the story from their own knowledge as much as possible.

If these simple points are followed this will make life easier for the person who is reviewing all this work. Unfortunately you may face an uphill struggle to get what you want as tying clients down to specifics can be an almost impossible task. Some landowners adopt a position where because they know and have intimately worked at the site they assume that everyone else should know the information that is in their head. Extracting that information and then presenting it is a logical and coherent manner is the most significant challenge facing applicants.

Let us now look at some of the matters an applicant might want to consider submitting as supporting evidence. There is usually a wealth of information that is potentially available. As with information for direct evidence it is again about considering what might be available and then ascertaining what is actually available.

Supporting Evidence

Maps and Plans

This can include old OS maps, plans from other applications on the site or building regulations applications. In some instances it might be worthwhile to have some plans drawn up so as to adequately show what parts of the site have been used for various activities.

Accounts/Business Records

Where a business use is alleged the starting point will be the annual accounts that have to be produced. Clearly some of these will be confidential. These records are a sure way of establishing, in appropriate cases, what has been undertaken on the site. If an applicant has used the same accountant for a long period of time then a statutory declaration corroborating the business use may be able to be produced. In many cases accountants will have to visit the site every few years to do a stock check thus putting them in a prime position to confirm what the applicant is alleging.

In some cases invoices for works carried out will be very telling. A lot of people will not want their private affairs put on a planning file. There are provisions in the access to information rules that assist here. If the information is genuinely personal it can be provided on a confidential basis. The fact that it has been provided can then be referred to in any statutory declarations. In one case recently the authors were able to provide copies of final accounts safe in the knowledge that they would not be disclosed further. In that case the information was provided subject to an undertaking from the council's solicitor that the information would only be made available to named individuals who would be considering the application and that it would not be included on the planning file. Such instances will, however, be the exception rather than the rule as the expectation has to be that all information is available for anyone interested in the application to see and comment upon.

Rating Records

It is one of the difficulties that seems to afflict the whole of the public sector that departments do not routinely share information with each other. The issue of data protection may be something that has to be considered but in the main there is a wealth of information available in publicly accessible documents.

As most applications will have an element of use involved a good starting point has to be whether or not the council has been collecting either council tax or business rates on the property. It is surprising that in a significant proportion of cases the council will have been collecting rates even though planning permission has not been obtained for the particular use. It should be remembered that the ability to levy rates or council tax does not depend upon any planning permission for the land. The council tax collectors are only concerned with what the actual use is so that they can then apply the appropriate levy.

In terms of evidence a letter from the relevant department confirming how long rates have been collected and the use on which that levy has been based can be attached to a statutory declaration as an exhibit.

Operating Licences

Certain businesses might need licences in order to trade. For example, the existence of a series of Operators Licences for a haulage depot should be sufficient to convince an authority that an applicant is telling the truth.

Depending upon the business there may be other regulatory requirements that can show what type of business and for how long it has operated from particular premises. For example, a solicitors practice will be regulated by the Law Society which will hold information as to how long the business has operated from particular premises.

In terms of presentation, copies of old licences or a letter from a regulator should be attached to statutory declarations.

Planning Files

As mentioned earlier there may be plans for different applications that may show that a building was existing at a point in time. Thus it will be necessary to consider examining the planning file not only for the actual site but maybe for adjoining sites as well. The file may contain other factual information that will be helpful. For example, in cases involving the non-discharge of a pre-commencement condition a letter on the planning file from the planning officer dealing with the application at the time to the effect that development has commenced but there is no record of the discharge of the relevant conditions will be incredibly helpful to an applicant. The local authority may not find such a letter as helpful but will nevertheless be bound by its contents in terms of the factual position.

Equally, it may the case that there is no such letter but there is also no evidence of any application having been made to discharge the relevant conditions. That is just as helpful as the planning file is supposed to be the record of the planning history of the site. In practice certain information may be missing as unfortunately local authorities went through a process of microfiching their planning files in the 1980's. This operation was undertaken by administrative staff with no planning experience. Cost was also an issue with the council paying for every document microfiched. It is not uncommon to come across a situation where there are almost identical plans but not all of them have been included in the microfiche. However, it is unusual to find correspondence missing as letters tend to be included in their entirety.

Paragraph 006 in the PPG says that *"a local planning authority always needs to cooperate with an applicant who is seeking information that the authority may hold about the planning status of the land."*

By way of contrast in a lot of cases the Council will not have any information at all. This is not necessarily a problem provided there is sufficient other information to support the application.

Other Information

Whilst people leave a so-called digital trail these days they will also have some form of living trail that can be helpful to an application. It is probably unrealistic to expect that an individual will have kept old utility bills etc for the relevant period of time. As with rating records it should be possible to obtain letters from utility providers, credit card companies and banks etc. They can confirm how long the account holder has been registered to a particular address. Such evidence can only be corroborative as it is of course possible that a person might have an accommodation address. However, if there is other evidence then such letters will help to form part of the overall picture.

It would be impossible to set out a complete list of potential sources of information as the available information will depend upon the nature of the application and the individual(s) providing information. However, the following should be considered;

Driving licences as they will contain a date of issue.

Log books for vehicles as they will have the date of acquisition shown.

Shotgun licences although a letter from the relevant police force may also be required to confirm the length of time the particular gun has been registered to the address.

Evidence of membership of certain groups or organisations.

Photographs that can be fixed in time. Some may have digital dates attached. In others, it may be possible to identify an individual in the photo and maybe the occasion or their age at the time. This can then be extrapolated to show that the relevant time period has expired.

Aerial or Google Earth photos. These can be useful but can also be limited as they usually involve a vertical perspective and can actually hide evidence because of this. This is particularly so where a use is being undertaken within a building or where there are trees on the site which can have the effect of shielding or hiding what is underneath their canopy.

The essential message to applicants would be to think around the issues and then think outside the box to see what might be available. The more supporting evidence that can be produced the more weight that can be given to the application.

Covering Letters

In some cases applicants or their agents will submit covering letters in support of their applications as they will not want to go to the trouble of paying for a corroborative declaration. These are usually the lines of "I have known the applicant for a long time and he is a good sort. He should have a certificate".

Their evidential value is not that great but they will occasionally contain some nuggets of information that will be useful to help determination of the application. This could assist with a refusal if they contradict the applicant.

Of more concern is a covering letter from agents. The authors take the view that an application should stand or fall on the evidence and if there is relevant information it should be put in the Statutory Declaration. Whilst it may be necessary to submit a covering letter to explain the application and draw all the documents together they should not be used to impart information that should form part of the evidence. Of particular concern are covering letters from agents that proceed on the premise "we are instructed that…" In other words the agents are not warranting that any of the information in the letter is correct.

Simple message, treat covering letters with caution.

Process

This can make or break an application. From the authors' perspective early and regular consultation with the council is vitally important. That does not mean that it will occur in all cases but where the case is strong getting some form of comment from the council will assist with the determination of the application. Prior to submitting anything if there is going to be a problem it will usually be best to speak to the Council solicitor. From everyone's point of view this can at least isolate the issues and can assist with swift processing of the application.

In some cases the draft Statutory Declarations can be submitted for comment. This can identify if there is anything more the Council wants covered. This will also speed up processing the application. The best that can be hoped for from the council is a qualified view as the Council cannot be asked to give a definitive view until the application has been submitted. In addition, the consultation exercise, if there is one, can throw up other information that could cast light on the applicant claim. Nevertheless this is useful exercise and will ultimately help all concerned with the process.

Consultation

There is no legal requirement to consult and there is varying practice about consultation. Paragraph 008 of the PPG says that it may be reasonable for the council to consider seeking information from parish councils, third parties and neighbours if they believe that "there is good reason to believe they may possess relevant information about the content of a specific application." This point was reiterated in the case of *France v Kensington and Chelsea Royal London Borough Council & Crown Estate Commissioners and Mr & Mrs Jonathan Hunt [2017] EWCA Civ 429.* The Court of Appeal went further and held that there was no legitimate expectation on the part of the claimant that it would be consulted or notified of an application.

But it must still be borne in mind that the Guidance states that it may nevertheless be reasonable for a local planning authority to seek evidence from these sources *"if there is good reason to believe they may possess relevant information about the content of a specific application"*, although it is expressly emphasised that any views expressed on the planning merits of the case are irrelevant to the determination of the application.

(The authors would note that the *France* case is also useful for countering the proposition, sometimes relied on by those contending that a certain development is not lawful, that lawfulness can only be established by obtaining a certificate, see at para. 52; *"the lawfulness of existing works is not dependent upon the existence of a section 191(1) certificate… it is a non sequitur to suggest that this is the only way in which a person may prove lawfulness for these purposes")*.

If parish councils are to be involved it is important send copies of the evidence to the Clerk early and get them to consider the application without waiting for the formal notice from the Council. Unfortunately parishes do not always provide the consultation response that is required as the members will think it is an application for planning permission rather than a factual exercise. Paragraph 8 continues "Views expressed by third parties on the planning merits of the case ..... are irrelevant when determining the application." Third parties in this instance will include parish councils. A covering letter to the Clerk explaining the nature of an application for a certificate of lawfulness and that only factual issues will be considered can sometimes pay dividends but do not be disappointed when it doesn't.

Neighbour consultation may happen whether the local planning authority want it or not as some neighbours, if the case is controversial, will become involved. Indeed the authors have known cases where neighbours have gone to the expense of providing their own Statutory Declarations so as to show that they mean business and want to be taken seriously.

One issue that will have to be considered by a local authority which does not routinely consult is the view the Ombudsman may decide if a complaint was made that a planning authority had deliberately failed to consult or had sought to exclude neighbours' evidence or information. This would also be relevant if there were a judicial review application.

So having waded through the morass of information made available it is now time to determine the application which is dealt with in the following chapter.

Summary

This chapter has been concerned with the issue of evidence. It has looked at the importance of evidence to the process and has suggested some potential sources of evidence to support an application and how that evidence should be presented. It also looks at the issue of consultation and the obligation placed on the local authority as to consultation.

CHECKLIST

1. Is the standard form to be used?

2. If not, does the application contain all the information required by section 191(5)?

3. What sources of evidence are potentially available?

4. Who will provide direct evidence and what will that comprise?

5. What supporting evidence is available and how will this be presented?

6. Is there a need for pre-application discussions with the council? If so, what issues are to be discussed? Is it the whole application or just the legal principles underpinning an application?

7. Is the evidence being presented properly? Do covering letters simply explain the application? Ensure they do not contain any evidence that should be contained in the statutory declarations.

CHAPTER FIVE

DETERMINING APPLICATIONS

As noted above, the key to a successful application must be the submission of a sufficiency of evidence to justify the grant of a certificate on the balance of probability that the development involved has become lawful.

Similarly, the PPG Guidance advises, see para. 17c-005, that an application

> *"must be accompanied by sufficient factual information/evidence for a local planning authority to decide the application... An application needs to describe precisely what is being applied for (not simply the use class) and the land to which the application relates. Without sufficient or precise information, a local planning authority may be justified in refusing a certificate. This does not preclude another application being submitted later on, if more information can be produced".*

Para. 17c-009 of the Guidance provides that in determining the application

> *"A local planning authority needs to consider whether, on the facts of the case and relevant planning law, the specific matter is or would be lawful".*

It further states that, if minded to grant a certificate, *"A local planning authority may choose to issue a lawful development certificate for a different description from that applied for [as permitted by section 191(4)] as an alternative to refusing a certificate altogether"*, although noting that it is nevertheless advisable to seek the applicant's agreement to any amendment before issuing the certificate.

Section 191(4) provides that

> *"(4) If, on an application under this section, the local planning authority are provided with information satisfying them of the lawfulness at the time of the application of the use, operations or other matter described in the application, or that description as modified by the local planning authority or a description substituted by them, they shall issue a certificate to that effect; and in any other case they shall refuse the application".*

A specific point to note on section 191(4) is that it refers to the local planning authority being satisfied as to the lawfulness of the development concerned *"at the time of the application"*. This is interpreted by some authorities as suggesting that an activity which is claimed to be lawful must always be actively being carried on at the date of the application for a certificate to be granted. This is however inconsistent with the general principle that lawfulness will accrue on expiry of the time period for taking enforcement action, see eg *Panton and Farmer [1999] 1 PLR 92* referred to above in which it was held that a lawful use right, once accrued, can only be lost by abandonment or some other means of supplanting a lawful use. Some support for the contrary approach where a breach of condition is concerned can be found in *Ellis* [2010] 1 P & CR 21 also referred to above.

As noted above, section 191(4) refers to the authority issuing a certificate in respect of the "*matter described in the application, or that description as modified by the local planning authority or a description substituted by them*". In relation to the latter it was held in *R (Freedman) v Wiltshire Council [2014] P.T.S.R. 696 that;*

> *"section 191(4) entitled a local planning authority, in principle, to substitute a different use from that described in the application; that the power was available to a planning authority where it was satisfied on the balance of probabilities that the evidence demonstrated that the use as substituted had been carried on continuously for a period of ten years or more; that the exercise of the power enabled any certificate granted accurately to reflect the actual existing lawful use".*

Para. 17c-009 of the Guidance makes the point that, in cases where the application is refused, "a refusal is not necessarily conclusive that something is not lawful, it may mean that to date insufficient evidence has been presented" in the application under consideration.

Where the certificate application is granted, the form in which a certificate is to be issued is prescribed in Schedule 8 of the DMPO.

Section 191(5) provides:

> *"(5) A certificate under this section shall—*
>
> *(a) specify the land to which it relates;*
>
> *(b) describe the use, operations or other matter in question (in the case of any use falling within one of the classes specified in an order under section 55(2)(f), identifying it by reference to that class);*
>
> *(c) give the reasons for determining the use, operations or other matter to be lawful; and*
>
> *(d) specify the date of the application for the certificate".*

Section 191(6) further provides that

> *"The lawfulness of any use, operations or other matter for which a certificate is in force under this section shall be conclusively presumed".*

It follows that care must be taken by the authority granting the certificate to ensure that its terms are appropriately precise. Para. 17c-010 of the Guidance warns that

> *"Precision in the terms of any certificate is vital, so there is no room for doubt about what was lawful at a particular date, as any subsequent change may be assessed against it".*

That paragraph continues

> *"It is important to note that:*
>
> - *a certificate for existing use must include a description of the use, operations or other matter for which it is granted regardless of whether the matters fall within a use class. But where it is within a "use class", a certificate must also specify the relevant "class". In all cases, the description needs to be more than simply a title or label, if future problems interpreting it are to be avoided. The certificate needs to therefore spell out the characteristics of the matter so as to define it unambiguously and with precision. This is particularly important for uses which do not fall within any "use class" (i.e. "sui generis" use); and*
>
> - *where a certificate is granted for one use on a "planning unit" which is in mixed or composite use, that situation may need to be carefully reflected in the certificate. Failure to do so may result in a loss of control over any subsequent intensification of the certificated use".*

The important points to note from the above are that, regardless of whether a use falls within a certain use class, the characteristics of the use need to be defined "unambiguously and with precision", as referred to in the first bullet point above. This is to ensure that the nature of what has been certified to represent what has historically and lawfully gone on on the land in question is specified sufficiently precisely so as to seek to ensure that problems do not arise in future in deciding whether any increase, variation or diversification of the activities on site involve a material change of use from the lawful use.

A similar point arises in the case of mixed or composite uses, as noted in the second bullet point above. If an element of that mixed or composite use is omitted from the uses certified to be lawful, the certified use could increase or expand in a manner causing greater impacts than would have been envisaged or desired when the certificate was granted.

Clearly, the authority has to be satisfied that it is judging a proposal against the correct planning unit, see eg Church Commissioners v. Secretary of State (1996) 71 P & CR 73 in which there was a debate about whether the appropriate unit against which to judge the materiality of a proposed change of use of a shop unit to a restaurant was the whole of the Gateshead Metro Centre or (as the court held) just the single unit itself. The recent case of *R (KP JR Management Co) v. Richmond LBC [2018] EWHC 84 (Admin)* confirms that the identification of the relevant planning unit is a matter for the judgement of the decision maker.

The fine-tuning of the extent and content of the certificate is provided for in section 193(4) which provides that a certificate may be granted *"(a) for the whole or part of the land specified in the application; and (b) where the application specifies two or more uses, operations or other matters, for all of them or some one or more of them".*

It is to be noted, however, that despite the desirability of a certificate being as specific as possible, there are two airfield cases which stand as examples where rather loose, general wording has nevertheless been held not to be unlawful. In *Tapp v. Thanet District Council [2001] EWCA Civ 559*, the Court of Appeal held that a CLOPUD relating to proposed use "as [an] airfield for civilian purposes" was not unduly vague, despite criticism that the local planning authority should have sought to define the use more restrictively so as to prevent the risk of intensification. Similarly, in *R (Wiltshire District Council) v. Cotswold District Council* [2009] EWHC 3702 (Admin) the court held a CLEUD relating to use for "general aviation purposes" was not too wide in its terms for the certificate to have been granted lawfully. Both cases nevertheless make the point that the local planning authority must be seen to have considered the issue of whether the terms of the certificate are sufficiently precise. These cases can be compared with *Hillingdon London Borough Council v. Secretary of State* [2008] EWHC 198 (Admin) in which it was held that the appropriate level of detail in the certificate will necessarily vary from case to case and the degree of particularisation is a matter of judgement for the decision-maker based on the evidence before them.

It is made clear in section 193(5) that a certificate "shall not affect any matter constituting a failure to comply with any condition or limitation subject to which planning permission has granted unless that matter is described in the certificate". As explained in the Guidance, para. 17c-011:

> *"A lawful development certificate may be granted on the basis that there is an extant planning permission for the development; however, that development still needs to comply with any conditions or limitations imposed on the development by that grant of permission, except to the extent specifically described in the lawful development certificate".*

The provisions governing the granting of CLOPUDs are slightly different from the terms of those governing CLEUDs, but the variations are logical having regard to the context of the exercise.

Certificate applications will often involve a question of construction of a permission or the terms of the GPDO or an assessment of the situation of the nature of a use being carried on on the ground against the nature of what is proposed where there may be a question whether any material change of use would be involved.

The Guidance suggests posing the question *"if this proposed change of use had occurred, or if this proposed operation had commenced, on the application date, would it have been lawful for planning purposes?"*, see para. 17c-009.

Section 192(2) provides:

> *"If, on an application under this section, the local planning authority are provided with information satisfying them that the use or operations described in the application would be lawful if instituted or begun at the time of the application, they shall issue a certificate to that effect; and in any other case they shall refuse the application".*

Section 192(3) is in identical terms to section 191(5) above, i.e. requiring that

> *"A certificate under this section shall*
>
> *(a) specify the land to which it relates;*
>
> *(b) describe the use or operations in question (in the case of any use falling within one of the classes specified in an order under section 55(2)(f), identifying it by reference to that class);*

(c) *give the reasons for determining the use or operations to be lawful; and*

(d) *specify the date of the application for the certificate".*

It is to be noted that section 192 does not contain any provision for modifying the description of development applied for. But Sullivan J as he then was in *Tapp v. Thanet DC* at first instance suggested that the authority might always bring about an appropriate modification by making it clear that an unmodified application would simply be refused.

Finally, the "conclusive presumption" provision for CLOPUDs is subject to the proviso of there being no material change of circumstances before the relevant activities commence, see section 192(4) as follows:

"The lawfulness of any use or operations for which a certificate is in force under this section shall be conclusively presumed unless there is a material change, before the use is instituted or the operations are begun, in any of the matters relevant to determining such lawfulness".

Summary

This chapter covers the formalities for determining applications by reference to the relevant provisions and guidance. It emphasises the need for particularity where the terms of a grant are concerned and refers to various other potential pitfalls in the application process.

CHECKLIST

For CLEUDs

1. Is the description of the development precise enough (especially in cases involving the use of land)?

2. Does the description in the application need modifying?

3. Is there sufficient evidence to decide the application?

4. Was the development lawful at the time of the application?

For CLOPUDs

1. Is the description of the development precise enough (especially in cases involving the use of land)?

2. Can it be modified if necessary (relying on *Tapp*)?

3. Pose the question "If the proposed change of use had occurred or the proposed development commenced on the application date would it have been lawful for planning purposes?

CHAPTER SIX

APPEALS

A right of appeal arises in two ways under section 195 of the 1990 Act. An appeal may be made to the Secretary of State where an application is:

(a) wholly or partly refused (including cases where the local planning authority issues a certificate in a different form); or

(b) not determined within the statutory eight-week period unless an extension has been agreed upon in writing.

Unlike other forms of appeal in planning matters there NO time limit for an appeal.

Making an Appeal

The Planning Portal contains very useful Guidance concerning the appeal process. Local authorities are exhorted to ensure that they have *"a sufficiently strong case…on the basis of the material before it."* Potential appellants are advised to ensure that they *"should be confident at the time they make their appeal that they have a clear case and do not need to rely on evidence that was not available to the local planning authority when it made its decision"*

The issue of costs is writ large across the guidance and both potential parties to an appeal would do well to bear this in mind. Equally the fact that the planning merits of an application have no relevance to an appeal is stressed. This is an issue more for local planning authorities who will often, for understandable reasons, be more motivated by the planning issues and consequences but that is not the correct starting point and could raise costs issues unnecessarily.

Determination of an Appeal

The criteria in Annex F for determining the most appropriate means of dealing with a planning appeal do not directly apply to appeals relating to lawful development certificates. However, the Guidance makes it clear that the criteria should be used and in the authors' view this is a sensible approach.

The most appropriate means of determination will to some extent depend upon the issues at stake. If there are issues of fact at stake then it is inevitable that a public inquiry will be necessary as the evidence will have to given on oath and be subjected to cross-examination. It is important to remember that evidence cannot be taken on oath at a Hearing.

If the issues are clear and the evidence is agreed but the issue is one of interpretation or legal submission it might be possible to deal with the issue simply by way of written representations.

Considerations For Appeal

This ties in to some extent with the considerations that will have to be applied when the actual decision is being taken. Thus, those who advise both sides will need to be evaluating not only the evidence but also the ability of those who will provide that evidence to stand up to cross-examination. As the evidence is pretty much set at the 9-week stage of any appeal (the point where any fresh evidence will be returned to the party who submits it unless there are exceptional circumstances) then an early consideration of where any gaps in the evidence might become apparent is an essential part of preparing for an appeal in these circumstances. Advocates should be engaged early and be given the opportunity to test the resilience of the witnesses in order to ensure that there are few, if any, surprises when it really matters at the Inquiry.

Third parties can be involved at the appeal. It is important to understand what it is they are likely to say and to ensure that they stick to facts as opposed to opinion as to the planning merits of the application. The Guidance makes it clear that third parties should do so but inevitably those with little experience of the process will inadvertently stray into the merits issues.

If the local authority is seeking to rely on the evidence provided by neighbours or those who made representations it is imperative that these witnesses are engaged at an early stage and given sufficient coaching to enable them to understand what the procedure will be and what the experience will be like. It would be a dangerous strategy for a local authority to seek to rely on these individuals turning up as third parties as there is no guarantee that they will in fact appear or that skillful cross examination will not undermine what they have to say. Add to this the requirement for the local authority to define its decision and it is not difficult to see a situation developing where an award of costs becomes a distinct possibility. A careful programme of engagement with witnesses, having decided who the local authority will call, is a must in order to ensure that a robust case can be presented.

As the planning merits are irrelevant to an appeal in these circumstances it follows that an Inspector cannot grant planning permission for the development unless there is a conjoined enforcement notice appeal that includes Ground A as one of the Grounds of Appeal.

Summary

This chapter has been concerned with the mechanics of an appeal and the practical considerations that flow from a decision to appeal. We offer a number of questions to ensure that both parties can ensure they present the best case possible.

CHECKLIST

1. Is an appeal appropriate?
2. What evidence/witnesses are available?
3. How reliable is the evidence/witnesses?
4. What is the appropriate means for determining the appeal?
5. What arrangements are in place for managing witnesses?

CHAPTER SEVEN

REVOCATION

Whilst it would be nice to think that everyone involved in the process will play by the rules the stakes are high as the issue of a certificate will have a significant effect on the value of land. If someone is sufficiently unscrupulous in their dealings with a local authority and seeks to actively mislead in circumstances where the local authority has no evidence to disprove or contradict the evidence advanced in support of an application the law will not permit them to profit from such unconscionable behaviour.

Section 193(7) gives a local planning authority the ability to revoke a certificate on one of two grounds namely;

(a) a statement was made or document used which was false in a material particular; or

(b) any material information was withheld

Subsection (8) provides that the procedure may be made by a development order. The current procedure is governed by Article 39 of The Town and Country Planning (Development Management and Procedure) (England) Order 2015 and in Wales the relevant order is the Town and Country Planning (Development Management Procedure) (Wales) Order 2012.

In both cases the procedure is the same. The decision as to whether or not to revoke is one for the local authority concerned. If a decision to revoke is made the procedure is as follows;

1) Notice of the proposal to revoke must be given to-

(a) the owner of the land affected;

(b) the occupier of the land affected;

(c) any other person who will in their opinion be affected by the revocation

(d) where the certificate was issued by the secretary of state or the Welsh ministers notice must be given to them

2) The notice must invite the person served to make representations to the proposal to revoke within 14 days of the date of service of the notice

3) The local planning authority may not revoke the certificate within the 14-day period

4) Any representations must then be considered and a decision made as to whether or not to continue with the proposed revocation

5) The decision must then be communicated to all those who were originally notified.

The principal point to bear in mind here is that the statement or information giving rise to the possibility of revocation must be "material". In the view of the authors this must be something more than just a simple inaccuracy. By using the word material Parliament has clearly set a higher threshold and this must mean that the statement made or information provided must have had a significant bearing on the outcome. This will impose a duty on the local authority to consider the evidence carefully and to decide whether or not the original application for a Certificate would have been refused had the true position been known. The Court in the case of *R (on the application of Mehta) v Kensington and Chelsea RLBC [2024] EWHC*

1986 (Admin) reinforced the point that the information must be first of "*false" or "misleading"* and secondly that it must be *"materially"* false and misleading thus confirming the view of the authors.

The case of *R (Ocado Retail Ltd) v Islington London Borough Council* [2021] P.T.S.R. 183 is also relevant here (and was followed in *Mehta*). In *Ocado* it was held that;

> *"(1) the first ground for revocation of a certificate of lawful use, in section 193(7)(a), laid down a straightforward, objective test that the statement or document relied upon was false, in the sense of incorrect, in a material particular;* section 193(7)(a) *did not additionally require that the party who made or relied upon the statement or document knew that it was false, or was reckless on that issue, or that the making of a statement was deliberately false or dishonest; similarly, the second ground for revocation in* section 193(7)(b) *imposed an objective test not dependent upon the applicant's subjective intention and the withholding of material information did not have to be deliberate;*
>
> *(2) That in considering whether information was false "in a material particular" or "material" information had been withheld, a local planning authority was entitled to consider the materiality of matters falling within* section 193(7)(a) and (b) of the 1990 Act *cumulatively as well as individually; that to be material the information in question had to be both relevant and significant, the falsity or withholding of which could, although not necessarily would, have resulted in the application for a lawful use certificate being refused or granted in different terms; that the materiality test might be satisfied where the relevant information could have resulted in the authority making a different factual finding (or drawing a different inference) to one made previously, or a line of inquiry leading to that outcome, which could have resulted in the application being determined differently; that while a local*

planning authority had to act on a correct understanding of relevant legal principles, the application of the law to the circumstances of the case was a matter for the authority, which involved an evaluative process of assessing the evidence submitted in support of an application for a lawful use certificate, weighing the material supplied along with any weaknesses or gaps in it, and making findings of fact and drawing inferences from that material, with the judgment of the decision-maker to be challenged only on rationality grounds; that where an authority identified a false statement or withheld information the essential legal question was whether its reasoning on why that matter was "material" was rationally incapable of supporting that judgment; that the grounds on which the power in section 193(7) to revoke was engaged were limited to those set out in paragraphs (a) and (b) and, like the initial decision whether to grant a certificate under section 191 , the planning merits of the matter in question were not relevant;

(3) if either paragraph (a) or (b) was met, section 193(7) of the 1990 Act conferred a discretion, not an obligation, on the local planning authority to revoke and, in deciding whether to do so, it could have regard to relevant factors in so far as it considered it appropriate to do so; that an authority's failure to take a particular consideration into account would not give rise to an error of law unless the consideration was "so obviously material" that it was irrational not to have taken it into account; that relevant factors could include the effect of revoking the certificate on affected landowners, particularly if time had elapsed and successors in title demonstrated the harm they would suffer, and whether a successor in title had been involved in or aware of the application for a certificate, particularly if it intended to rely upon any certificate granted; that where a local authority had reason to conclude that material information had been deliberately withheld at the application stage, or that there had been material concealment of information after the certificate was issued, those matters could be

taken into account as weighing in favour of revocation; that, furthermore, although the planning merits of a development or a legitimised breach of condition were irrelevant to whether paragraphs (a) or (b) of section 193(7) were satisfied, a local authority could have regard to that aspect when exercising its discretion whether to revoke a certificate, although it was entirely a matter for the authority whether to consider planning benefits or harm at all and, if so, to what extent, subject only to review on the grounds of irrationality;

(4) the impact of section 193(7) on the CLEUD process is that an applicant assumes a risk (which passes to or affects successors in title) that any certificate he obtains may be revoked if it turns out that materially inadequate or false information was provided on the application. That risk is likely to be greater if he takes a minimalist approach to the provision of information. In practical terms, an applicant takes on responsibility for supplying information to verify his application that will not give rise to action under section 193(7)."

If a Certificate is revoked the land may be subject to immediate enforcement action although there is nothing to preclude a further application being made. In such a case a little more skepticism may be evident in the approach of the local authority as to the evidence. No compensation is payable following a decision to revoke.

In terms of how to get it wrong the case of *R v Surrey CC ex p Bridge Court Holdings Ltd QBD (Potts J) 16/2 2000 (CO/4011/1998)* is a perfect example. In that case not only did the council fail to inform the owner of the land of the intention to revoke it also failed to identify or specify the statements or information which were said to be false. Indeed the committee report that sought authority acknowledged that further investigation would be required before revoking. Despite this the council still decided to proceed. A salutary lesson for those contemplating such a draconian step but it is just as easy to get it right if the procedure is properly followed.

Summary

This section has been concerned with revocation. This is not a common occurrence and it is for that reason that if a local authority is contemplating embarking upon this path it must ensure that it gets the procedure correct.

CHECKLIST

1. What statements or information are considered to be false?
2. Are they material?
3. What interests in terms of ownership or occupation exist?
4. Prepare notice of intention to revoke and specify the statements or information considered to be false and why they are material
5. Invite representations and give 14 days for receipt. Remember to allow for service days for post etc.
6. Consider representations and make final decision.
7. Inform those identified at point 3 of the decision.

CHAPTER EIGHT

CERTIFICATES OF LAWFULNESS OF PROPOSED USE OR DEVELOPMENT UNDER SECTION 192 OR "CLOPUDS"

Unlike certificates under section 192, certificates under section 191 are concerned with "existing" development i.e. what is in place or is going on already and whether that is lawful or not. Applications under section 192 for certificates of lawfulness of proposed use or development, known as CLOPUDS, are concerned with something which has not happened yet but which requires a determination as to its lawfulness if it occurred.

As stated in the PPG Guidance para. 17c-009, the local planning authority needs to pose itself the question in considering a CLOPUD application:

> *"If this proposed change of use had occurred, or if this proposed operation had commenced, on the application date, would it have been lawful for planning purposes?"*

This question may arise in the context of a site with a planning history comprising grants of planning permission, extant enforcement notices and even certificates of lawfulness. But the question still only applies to proposals, i.e. operations or changes of use that have not yet occurred. This can sometimes cause difficulties for local authorities when confronted with certain types of application. The authors have recently been involved in a number of cases where an application for a CLOPUD has been made to establish whether or not a permission can be built out. In those cases acts of commencement had been undertaken following discharge of the relevant pre-commencement conditions and evidence showing that a foundation trench had been excavated in the correct position was submitted with the application.

In both cases the authorities erroneously took the view that a CLOPUD was not the appropriate means to establish whether or not it would be lawful to complete the dwelling. The view expressed was that an application for a CLEUD should be submitted to establish the lawfulness of the trench works. That was the wrong way to approach the matter as even if a CLEUD was issued for the trench works there would still be a need to establish if the permission could be built out.

The ability to use the CLOPUD this procedure to establish lawfulness in these cases was established in the case of *France v Kensington and Chelsea Royal London Borough Council & Crown Estate Commissioners and Mr & Mrs Jonathan Hunt [2017] EWCA Civ 429* previously mentioned in the chapter on consultation. This is an important point to bear in mind when considering how to establish if an extant permission is still valid and capable of being built out.

As with CLEUD applications under section 191, the planning merits are not relevant to the local planning authority's determination. But the authority must also consider whether a proposal would involve a breach of any existing condition which might affect the lawfulness of the proposed development, see section 193(5).

The applicant of course needs to describe their proposal sufficiently clearly and precisely so that the authority can understand exactly what is proposed for consideration.

If the authority is provided with information satisfying them that the use or operations described in the application would be lawful if instituted or begun at the time of the application, they will issue a certificate to that effect but in any other case they will refuse the application, see section 191(2).

As with CLEUD applications, the authority may wish to vary the description of the proposed development as an alternative to refusing the application. But the Guidance states that it is advisable for them to seek the applicant's agreement to any amendment, see again para. 17c-009.

It is to be noted that there is no equivalent provision in section 192 to section 191(4) which expressly allows the authority to modify or substitute the description. So approaching the applicant provides a way of getting round the problem identified by Sullivan J in *R v. Thanet DC ex parte Tapp (2001) 82 P & CR 520* that no such power can be implied, see para. [50] (Sullivan J's conclusion was upheld on appeal, see *[2002] P & CR 7* at para. [18]). Sullivan J suggested that (depending on the circumstances) the authority might reply to the applicant on these lines, see para. [51]:

> *"Your description of the proposed use is so general that it admits of intensification which may be of such a scale as to change the character of the use, therefore we will not be able to be satisfied for the purposes of section 192(2) that it will be lawful and will have to refuse your application as it stands. If, however, you are prepared to amend the description of the proposed development to say, caravan site for 12 touring caravans or haulage yard for 12 HGVs, we will then be able to grant you a certificate, because we will be able to be satisfied that such a proposed use will be lawful."*

It follows that an authority should be cautious about modifying an applicant's description of development unilaterally, despite the apparently open-ended terms of the Guidance in para. 17c-009:

> *"A local planning authority may choose to issue a lawful development certificate for a different description from that applied for as an alternative to refusing a certificate altogether..."*

The formalities for an application under section 191 are set out in art. 39 of the Development Management Procedure Order 2015. Art. 39(1) requires the applicant to use the application form published by the Secretary of State (or a form substantially to the same effect) and to specify on it the land to which the application relates, describe the use, operations or other matter in question (and include the particulars specified or referred to in the form).

Art. 39(2) further provides:

> "(2) *An application to which paragraph (1) applies must be accompanied by*
>
> > *(a) a plan identifying the land to which the application relates drawn to an identified scale and showing the direction of North;*
> >
> > *(b) such evidence verifying the information included in the application as the applicant can provide; and*
> >
> > *(c) a statement setting out the applicant's interest in the land, the name and address of any other person known to the applicant to have an interest in the land and whether any such other person has been notified of the application*".

As provided in section 192(3), any certificate which is ultimately granted has to:

> *(1) specify the land to which it relates;*
>
> *(2) describe the use or operations in question (and in the case of any use falling within one of the use classes specified in the Use Classes Order, identifying it by reference to that use class);*

(3) give the reasons for determining the use or operations to be lawful; and

(4) specify the date of the application for the certificate.

Section 193(4) applies so that a certificate may be granted *"(a) for the whole or part of the land specified in the application; and (b) where the application specifies two or more uses, operations or other matters, for all of them or some one or more of them".*

Clearly, the authority has to be satisfied that it is judging a proposal against the correct planning unit, see eg *Church Commissioners v. Secretary of State (1996) 71 P & CR 73* in which there was a debate about whether the appropriate unit against which to judge the materiality of a proposed change of use of a shop unit to a restaurant was the whole of the Gateshead Metro Centre or (as the court held) just the single unit itself. The recent case of *R (KP JR Management Co) v. Richmond LBC [2018] EWHC 84 (Admin)* confirms that the identification of the relevant planning unit is a matter for the judgement of the decision maker.

Section 192(4) contains a similar provision to that in section 191(6) as the conclusiveness of a certificate once granted. But it is importantly qualified by reference to the effect of a material change of circumstances before the proposal is put into effect so that a certificate will no longer sanction the applicant's proposal if such a material change occurs:

> *"(4) The lawfulness of any use or operations for which a certificate is in force under this section shall be conclusively presumed unless there is a material change, before the use is instituted or the operations are begun, in any of the matters relevant to determining such lawfulness".*

The former guidance in Circular 10/97 gave as "obvious examples" of such a material change of the making of an Article 4 direction taking away permitted development rights or some other change to permitted development rights or the revocation of a planning permission on which the application relied, see para. 8.30. The former guidance went on to say that, so long as the use concerned had been instituted or the operations begun at the time of the material change occurred, then the development could lawfully continue.

Summary

This chapter has been concerned with the issue of proposed use or development and the considerations that apply to applications relating to such issues. It draws attention to the relevant practical issues that have to be dealt with in this scenario.

CHECKLIST

1. What is the nature of the proposed development?
2. Has the use been instituted or have operations already commenced? If so, the applicant should apply under section 191.
3. Pose the question: "If this proposed change of use had occurred, or if this proposed operation had commenced, on the application date, would it have been lawful for planning purposes?"
4. Is there any relevant planning history (planning permissions, enforcement notices or LDCs)?
5. In particular, are there any planning conditions which might affect the proposal?
6. Is the proposal defined sufficiently clearly and precisely to make a decision?
7. Does the description of the proposed development need modifying or substituting (and, if so, will the applicant agree to that)?
8. Should the certificate be granted on only part of the land in the application or for only some uses and not others?
9. Has the applicant identified the correct planning unit?
10. Is the application seeking to establish the validity of an extant permission? If so, be alert to the France v Kensington and Chelsea provisions.

CHAPTER NINE

LISTED BUILDINGS AND CERTIFICATES OF LAWFULNESS

Provisions were inserted into the Planning (Listed Buildings and Conservation Areas) act 1990 to enable the owner of a listed building to ascertain whether or not proposed works would be lawful. In essence the provisions in sections 26H to 26K provide a procedure comparable to that for a CLOPUD. Unlike development under the Town and Country Planning Act 1990 which can become immune from enforcement action there are no equivalent provisions relating to works that have been undertaken to listed buildings. This can be a significant issue where due diligence is being undertaken as part of the purchase of a listed building. Often purchasers and vendors will need to remain silent on the point especially if the works were undertaken recently. Whilst the risk of prosecution may not be a significant issue as only those who have undertaken the works can be prosecuted the possibility of a listed building enforcement notice with the attendant cost of putting right that which affects the building should be more of a concern.

An application under section 26H must specify the building and describe the works. Subsection (2) provides that "works would be lawful if they would not affect the character of the listed building as a building of special architectural or historic interest." In the case of *France and Kensington and Chelsea* that we mentioned in relation to consultation the court held that section 26 H was primarily aimed at the many vases where alterations were so small that they could not arguably affect the character if the building. In these cases the procedure allowed owners to ascertain if they could proceed without the need to apply for listed building consent.

The Court of Appeal also stressed that such applications could only apply to "prospective" works and could not be used to justify the lawfulness of works already undertaken.

Subsection (3) imposes a duty on a local authority to issue a certificate where information has been provided to them that the works described in the application would be lawful.

There are procedural requirements set out in subsection (4) as to what a certificate must contain. Thus, a certificate must;

1. specify the building to which it relates;
2. describe the works concerned;
3. give the reasons for determining that the works would be lawful;
4. specify the date of the issue of the certificate.

Once issued a certificate conclusively presumes that the works specified in it are lawful provided they are carried out within 10 years of the date of the certificate and the certificate has not been revoked.

Section 26 I contains supplementary provisions as to the application process. Regulation making powers are reserved to the Secretary of State who can specify requirement which are similar to those which apply to normal certificate applications. As with applications for a CLOPUD the local authority may determine that the certificate applies to a lesser area than that applied for or for lesser works than those specified in the application.

Various regulations have been made which largely mirror the requirements for CLOPUDS with a number of differences, For example, the time period for determination of the application is 6 weeks from the date of application although there is provision to extend the time period of notice of appeal has been given to the Secretary of State. In that scenario the time limit can be extended for such period as is agreed between the applicant and the local authority. See Regulation 2 (5) (b) of the Planning (Listed Buildings) (Certificates of lawfulness of Proposed Works) Regulations 2014.

Appeal against Refusal of Certificate

The time limit for appealing is 6 months from the date of decision or if it is a non-determination appeal within 6 months of the expiry of the time period for determination. In most cases this will be the 6-week period allowed for the local authority to determine the application.

A similar duty is placed on the Secretary of State to issue a certificate if satisfied that the works will not affect the listed building or its character. Given the technical nature of such applications there will no doubt be a certain amount of opinion evidence that will form part of the application and any appeal. Experts on both sides will no doubt have views that may not always coincide as to what effect, if any, the works will have on the listed building.

This should be contrasted with a CLOPUD application which will be more of a factual/legal exercise as to whether or not the works would be lawful. In the case of listed buildings the outcome will be determined more by opinion and experience of the decision maker based on an assessment as to whether or not there is an impact on the listed building. Applications and appeals will therefore be more akin to planning applications in many ways as opposed to the factual basis for determining CLEUD and CLOPUD applications and appeals. This will make the outcome of such appeals much more uncertain and more difficult for both parties to argue.

Revocation of a Certificate

Similar provisions apply here as with CLOPUDS and CLEUDS. The starting point is section 26 I (6). The grounds are the same as for CLOPUDS in that a statement must have been made that was *"false in a material particular"* or *"material information was withheld."* Once again attention is drawn to the need for the statement or the material withheld to be "material" thus imposing the higher standard such that the decision would have been different had the correct position have been known.

The procedural requirements are similar although when notice of intended revocation is served a minimum of 14 days has to be given for representations to be made.

Summary

This chapter has been concerned with the provisions relating to proposed works to listed buildings and how to obtain a certificate that enables the works to be undertaken without the need for listed building consent. It is important to be clear that there is no period for immunity for works undertaken to a listed building which can be enforced against without limit of time. The provisions discussed in this chapter only relate to proposed works.

CHECKLIST

1. What works are proposed?
2. Do they affect the special architectural character of the building?
3. Do they affect the historical interest of the building?
4. What evidence is to be presented?
5. Is expert evidence required?
6. What is the source of such evidence?
7. If an appeal is to be pursued how strong is the expert evidence.
8. If a Certificate is to be revoked ensure the proper procedure is followed.

CHAPTER TEN

CARAVANS AND MOBILE HOMES

It is with some trepidation that the authors embark on a consideration of this issue given the potential problems and difficulties that may arise. Nevertheless, there are many difficult sites that exist around the country and both local authorities and landowners struggle on a daily basis to resolve what are sometimes conflicting considerations.

Let us, therefore start at the beginning.

What Constitutes a Caravan

"Caravan" is defined in section 29 of the Caravan Sites and Control of Development Act 1960 as follows;

> *"… Any structure designed or adapted for human habitation which is capable of being moved from one place to another (whether being towed, or by being transported on a motor vehicle or trailer) and any motor vehicle so designed or adapted but does not include*
>
> *(A) Any railway rolling stock which is for the time being on rails forming part of a system, or (B) Any tent"*

Section 13 of the Caravan Sites Act 1968 brings the definition of twin unit caravans within the definition of caravan in the 1960 Act.

The definition in section 13 is as follows;

> *"1. A structure designed or adapted for human habitation which:-*

> *(a) is composed of not more than two sections separately constructed and designed to be assembled on a site by means of bolts, clamps or other devices; and*
>
> *(b) is, when assembled, physically capable of being moved by road from one place to another (whether by being towed, or by being transported on a motor vehicle or trailer),…"*

It is necessary to go through this definition in some detail and to refer to some relevant case law concerning this section.

Subsection 1 (a) clearly envisages that the unit must be constructed in no more than two pieces and then assembled on site. This is reinforced when the provisions of subsection (b) are considered. This requires that the unit so assembled has to be "physically capable of being moved by road from one place to another (whether by being towed, or by being transported on a motor vehicle or trailer),…". In this regard the case of *Sam Odina and Chantal Launay v Mackland Limited [2009] 5 WLUK 622* is highly relevant. That case established that if a unit has to be disassembled into more than two sections it cannot fall within the definition of mobile home. It also establishes that if the structure is too wide to be lawfully moved on the public highway it is outwith the definition.

This is further reinforced by the case of *Bury Metropolitan Borough Council v Secretary of State for Communities and Local Government and Gary Entwistle [2011] EWHC 2192.* The principal point to take from this case is that the unit has to be capable of being "lawfully" moved on a public highway following its assembly.

As can be seen there is somewhat of a minefield to be navigated here and the complexity only increases when one starts to consider other matters that frequently arise.

By far the biggest issue is when extensions are attached to the original caravan or mobile home. In *Odina* the judge opined that if the original mobile home was extended and hen comprised more than 2 pieces then it could not be regarded as falling within the definition of caravan in the Acts.

In a recent appeal decision that the authors were involved in an enforcement notice was quashed on the basis that various extensions that had been attached to the mobile homes took them outside of the definition. The Decision Notice concerns multiple appeals on the same site. For ease of reference we will use the first reference number *APP/K2610/C/23/3322357.* The Inspector recited the facts in each case and recorded that some had substantial projecting canopies supported by external posts and that these posts were integral to the decking that had been constructed under the canopies. In other cases he concluded that the units could not be moved without the possibility of significant structural damage and did not, therefore, fall within the definition in the Acts. As can be seen it is important to be clear as to what is actually on site and whether or not the relevant limbs of the statutory definition are fulfilled. In some cases this will inevitably lead to the need for expert advice to ensure that the decision maker has actual evidence as opposed to opinion or speculation in order to arrive at a robust decision.

Extent of Permitted Uses

As we discussed in the chapter on Determination of applications the actual wording used in either planning permissions or Certificates of Lawfulness can lead to unintended consequences. In the case of *Breckland DC v Secretary of State for Housing communities and Local Government 2020] EWHC 292 (Admin)* the Court held that the fact that a caravan park and campsite had been used only for touring caravans by holidaymakers did not mean that the words "use of land as a caravan and camping site" in a CLEUD restricted the use of the site to temporary caravan stays for holiday purposes. The statutory definition of "caravan" applied to the CLEUD and it included mobile homes for permanent occupation.

This should be contrasted with the case of *Barton Park Estates Ltd v Secretary of State for Housing Communities and Local Government* [2022] EWCA Civ 833 21 where the court of Appeal decided that a proposal to station up to 80 caravans "for the purposes of human habitation" on a caravan site which had planning permission for a specific mix of residential and holiday units fell outside the scope of that planning permission and represented a material change of use.

Once again we urge decision makers to think carefully before they press print on planning permissions.

CHECKLIST

1. Is the structure a caravan within the definition in the 1960 Act?

2. Is it a twin structure within the definition in the 1968 Act?

3. Have all the relevant parts of the definition(s) been satisfied?

4. Have any extensions or other appendages been attached to the unit?

5. What is the effect of such additions and do they take the unit outside the definition?

‘The Electronic Communications Code: A Practical Guide – Second Edition’ by Kerry Bretherton KC, James Castle, Mark Loveday
‘A Practical Guide to the Independent School Standards – September 2023 Edition’ by Sarah McKimm
'A Practical Guide to Estate Administration and Crypto Assets' by Richard Marshall
‘A Practical Guide to Parental Alienation in Private and Public Law Children Cases’ by Sam King QC & Frankie Shama
‘Contested Heritage – Removing Art from Land and Historic Buildings’ by Richard Harwood QC, Catherine Dobson, David Sawtell
‘The Limits of Separate Legal Personality: When Those Running a Company Can Be Held Personally Liable for Losses Caused to Third Parties Outside of the Company’ by Dr Mike Wilkinson
‘A Practical Guide to Transgender Law’ by Robin Moira White & Nicola Newbegin
‘A Practical Guide to ‘Stranded Spouses’ in Family Law’ by Mani Singh Basi
‘A Practical Guide to Residential Freehold Conveyancing’ by Lorraine Richardson
‘A Practical Guide to Pensions on Divorce for Lawyers’ by Bryan Scant
‘A Practical Guide to Challenging Sham Marriage Allegations in Immigration Law’ by Priya Solanki
‘A Practical Guide to Digital Communications Evidence in Criminal Law’ by Sam Willis
‘A Practical Guide to Legal Rights in Scotland’ by Sarah-Jane Macdonald
‘A Practical Guide to New Build Conveyancing’ by Paul Sams & Rebecca East
‘A Practical Guide to Inherited Wealth on Divorce’ by Hayley Trim
‘A Practical Guide to Practice Direction 12J and Domestic Abuse in Private Law Children Proceedings’ by Rebecca Cross & Malvika Jaganmohan
‘A Practical Guide to Confiscation and Restraint’ by Narita Bahra QC, John Carl Townsend, David Winch
‘A Practical Guide to the Law of Forests in Scotland’ by Philip Buchan
‘A Practical Guide to Health and Medical Cases in Immigration Law’ by Rebecca Chapman & Miranda Butler
‘A Practical Guide to Bad Character Evidence for Criminal Practitioners by Aparna Rao
‘A Practical Guide to Extradition Law post-Brexit’ by Myles Grandison et al
‘A Practical Guide to Hoarding and Mental Health for Housing Lawyers’ by Rachel Coyle

'Stephens on Contractual Indemnities' by Richard Stephens
'A Practical Guide to the EU Succession Regulation' by Richard Frimston
'A Practical Guide to Solicitor and Client Costs – Second Edition' by Robin Dunne
'Constructive Dismissal – Practice Pointers and Principles' by Benjimin Burgher
'A Practical Guide to Religion and Belief Discrimination Claims in the Workplace' by Kashif Ali
'A Practical Guide to the Law of Medical Treatment Decisions' by Ben Troke
'Fundamental Dishonesty and QOCS in Personal Injury Proceedings: Law and Practice' by Jake Rowley
'A Practical Guide to the Law in Relation to School Exclusions' by Charlotte Hadfield & Alice de Coverley
'A Practical Guide to Divorce for the Silver Separators' by Karin Walker
'The Right to be Forgotten – The Law and Practical Issues' by Melissa Stock
'A Practical Guide to Planning Law and Rights of Way in National Parks, the Broads and AONBs' by James Maurici QC, James Neill et al
'A Practical Guide to Election Law' by Tom Tabori
'A Practical Guide to the Law in Relation to Surrogacy' by Andrew Powell
'A Practical Guide to Claims Arising from Fatal Accidents – Second Edition' by James Patience
'A Practical Guide to Asbestos Claims' by Jonathan Owen & Gareth McAloon
'A Practical Guide to Stamp Duty Land Tax in England and Northern Ireland' by Suzanne O'Hara
'A Practical Guide to the Law of Farming Partnerships' by Philip Whitcomb
'A Practical Guide to the Law of Unlawful Eviction and Harassment – Second Edition' by Stephanie Lovegrove
'A Practical Guide to Costs in Personal Injury Claims – Second Edition' by Matthew Hoe
'A Practical Guide to the General Data Protection Regulation (GDPR) – Second Edition' by Keith Markham
'A Practical Guide to Working with Litigants in Person and McKenzie Friends in Family Cases' by Stuart Barlow
'Protecting Unregistered Brands: A Practical Guide to the Law of Passing Off' by Lorna Brazell
'A Practical Guide to Secondary Liability and Joint Enterprise Post-Jogee' by Joanne Cecil & James Mehigan

'A Practical Guide to the Pre-Action RTA Claims Protocol for Personal Injury Lawyers' by Antonia Ford

'A Practical Guide to Neighbour Disputes and the Law' by Alexander Walsh

'A Practical Guide to Coercive Control for Legal Practitioners and Victims' by Rachel Horman

'A Practical Guide to the Law of Driverless Cars – Second Edition'

by Alex Glassbrook, Emma Northey & Scarlett Milligan

'A Practical Guide to TOLATA Claims' by Greg Williams

'A Practical Guide to Elderly Law – Second Edition' by Justin Patten

'A Practical Guide to Responding to Housing Disrepair and Unfitness Claims' by Iain Wightwick

'A Practical Guide to the Law of Bullying and Harassment in the Workplace' by Philip Hyland

'How to Be a Freelance Solicitor: A Practical Guide to the SRA-Regulated Freelance Solicitor Model' by Paul Bennett

'A Practical Guide to Prison Injury Claims' by Malcolm Johnson

'A Practical Guide to Advising Clients at the Police Station' by Colin Stephen McKeown-Beaumont

'A Practical Guide to Antisocial Behaviour Injunctions – Second Edition' by Iain Wightwick

'Practical Mediation: A Guide for Mediators, Advocates, Advisers, Lawyers, and Students in Civil, Commercial, Business, Property, Workplace, and Employment Cases' by Jonathan Dingle with John Sephton

'The Mini-Pupillage Workbook' by David Boyle

'A Practical Guide to Crofting Law' by Brian Inkster

'A Practical Guide to the Law of Domain Names and Cybersquatting' by Andrew Clemson

'A Practical Guide to the Law of Gender Pay Gap Reporting' by Harini Iyengar

'NHS Whistleblowing and the Law' by Joseph England

'Employment Law and the Gig Economy' by Nigel Mackay & Annie Powell

'A Practical Guide to Noise Induced Hearing Loss (NIHL) Claims' by Andrew Mckie, Ian Skeate, Gareth McAloon

'An Introduction to Beauty Negligence Claims – A Practical Guide for the Personal Injury Practitioner' by Greg Almond

'Intercompany Agreements for Transfer Pricing Compliance' by Paul Sutton

'Zen and the Art of Mediation' by Martin Plowman

'A Practical Guide to Adoption for Family Lawyers' by Graham Pegg

'A Practical Guide to Industrial Disease Claims' by Andrew Mckie & Ian Skeate
'A Practical Guide to Conducting a Sheriff Court Proof' by Andrew Stevenson
'A Practical Guide to Vicarious Liability' by Mariel Irvine
'A Practical Guide to Applications for Landlord's Consent and Variation of Leases' by Mark Shelton
'A Practical Guide to Relief from Sanctions Post-Mitchell and Denton' by Peter Causton
'A Practical Guide to Equity Release for Advisors' by Paul Sams
'A Practical Guide to Financial Services Claims' by Chris Hegarty
'A Practical Guide to Financial Ombudsman Service Claims' by Adam Temple & Robert Scrivenor
'A Practical Guide to Running Housing Disrepair and Cavity Wall Claims – Second Edition' by Andrew Mckie & Ian Skeate
'A Practical Guide to Holiday Sickness Claims – Second Edition' by Andrew Mckie & Ian Skeate
'Arguments and Tactics for Personal Injury and Clinical Negligence Claims' by Dorian Williams
'A Practical Guide to Drone Law' by Rufus Ballaster, Andrew Firman, Eleanor Clot
'On Experts: CPR35 for Lawyers and Experts' by David Boyle
'An Introduction to Personal Injury Law' by David Boyle

www.ingramcontent.com/pod-product-compliance
Lightning Source LLC
LaVergne TN
LVHW021113300926
849160LV00009B/713
9781916698512